KING'S CROSS
STATION
THROUGH TIME
John Christopher

AMBERLEY PUBLISHING

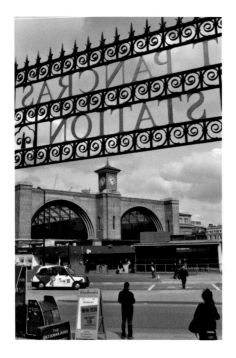

Left: Close neighbours, the front of King's Cross seen through the archway leading up to the forecourt of the St Pancras hotel.

About this book

The illustrations in this book encourage the reader to explore many aspects of King's Cross Station. They seek to document not only its history, its architecture and the changes that have occurred over the years, but also record the day-to-day life of this important railway terminus. Hopefully it will encourage you to delve a little deeper when exploring the station and its environs, but please note that public access and photography is sometimes restricted for reasons of safety and security.

First published 2012

Amberley Publishing
The Hill, Stroud
Gloucestershire, GL5 4EP

www.amberley-books.com

Copyright © John Christopher, 2012

The right of John Christopher to be identified as the Author of this work has been asserted in accordance with the Copyrights, Designs and Patents Act 1988.

ISBN 978 1 4456 0530 2

British Library Cataloguing in Publication Data.
A catalogue record for this book is available from the British Library.

Typeset in 9.5pt on 12pt Celeste.
Typesetting by Amberley Publishing.
Printed in the UK.

Introduction

Through a combination of design and more than a modicum of good fortune King's Cross Station has survived for more than a century and a half intact and, against the odds, has become, in my opinion, the most unspoilt and finest of all of London's great railway termini. But it hasn't always been appreciated as such and for most of its life King's Cross has been over-shadowed by its ostentatious neighbour, St Pancras.

King's Cross Station dates from the mid-period of railway arrivals in London during the nineteenth century (and some sixteen years before St Pancras came on the scene). At the time of its construction the area to the south of the New Road, which ran roughly from Paddington in the west up to Islington – the central section as far as the junction with Pentonville Road was renamed as Euston Road in 1852 – had already been thoroughly developed as high quality housing. Furthermore, in 1846 the Royal Commission on Railway Termini attempted to ring-fence central London, protecting it from invasive major railway construction, by limiting all new works to the north side of the road. Thus we have five major termini, Paddington, Marylebone, Euston, St Pancras and King's Cross, strung out in a line along the Euston Road. When it came to bringing the Great Northern Railway's east coast line into the capital, the company's engineers selected a site at the eastern end of Euston Road.

The area was known as King's Cross and took its name from a short-lived monument which was erected in 1836 to honour the late King George VI, but dismantled only nine years later. The land was mostly open fields at the time although it did include the Smallpox Hospital, which was demolished to make way for the station. In many respects this was a less than ideal location as the Regent's Canal was only 600 feet (183 m) or so from the end of the station, and ran east–west 30 ft (9.1 m) above the level of the platforms. Sir William Cubitt and his son Joseph were put in charge of designing the station and their solution

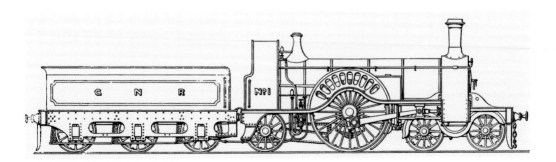

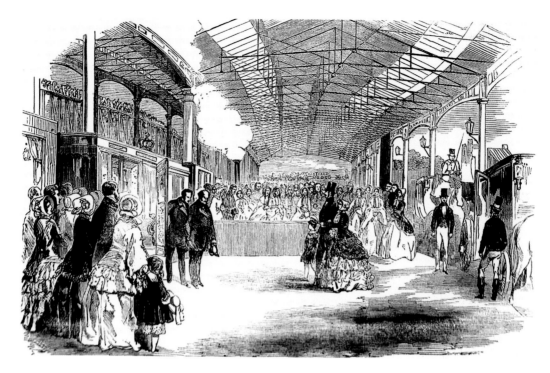

A goods station fit for a Queen

While King's Cross was under construction a temporary terminus was opened on the edge of the Goods Station to the west of Maiden Lane (now York Way). Queen Victoria departed from here on a trip to Scotland in 1851. That structure has gone although the horizontal spandrels, seen to the left of the upper picture, remain on the right-hand side of the Handyside Roof which was built alongside in 1888.

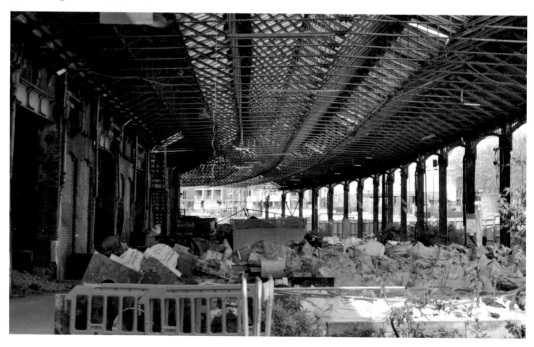

was to take the railway underneath the canal, dipping slightly through the Gas Works Tunnel and then up a gradient of 1 in 107 through the Copenhagen Tunnel.

The architect for the station building was yet another Cubitt, this time Joseph, the nephew of Sir William, who produced a design featuring a double-span arched roof. At 800 feet (244 m) long it was to be the largest station in the capital as it was 100 feet (30 m) longer than Brunel's triple arches of iron and glass being built at Paddington at around the same time. Cubitt's spans were also much wider at 105 feet (32 m) across and he bucked the latest trend in building with iron in favour of laminated timber ribs spaced at 20-foot (6-m) intervals. The ribs were supported on iron shoes attached to the two side walls and a dividing wall which ran down the middle of the station. Their thrust was taken by the office block on the western side and by wooden buttresses above a cab drive on the eastern side. The buttresses were later replaced by an additional storey of offices over the cab drive.

King's Cross lacked the more usual hotel block that provided a frontage to several of London's other stations and instead the bold no-frills façade consisted of a screen wall of London stock brick, divided vertically into two sections with each one pierced by large semicircular windows known as 'lunettes' to reveal and mimic the roofs within. 'The building will depend for its effect on the largeness of some of the features, its fitness for its purpose and its characteristic expression of that purpose,' claimed Lewis Cubitt. The terminus opened for business on 14 October 1852, and while the *Illustrated London News* said that it presented an 'imposing appearance', *The Builder* went further, saying that 'great plainness prevails'. In other words the Victorians didn't know what to make of it. They weren't quite ready for the stark, simple lines which served as a refreshing foil to the overblown decorative and sham Gothic that pervades so many of London's major nineteenth-century buildings. Exuding functionality and a rare degree of architectural integrity, the station looks, even now, or perhaps especially now, extraordinarily modern.

While King's Cross was still under construction a temporary station was erected in August 1850 alongside the goods station to the west of Maiden Lane (now known as York Way). It ran parallel to the surviving curved roof which stands beside the Midland Shed and although this roof is a later addition dating from 1888, it does retain the horizontal iron spandrels from the now demolished 1850 station roof. See page 4.

When the main King's Cross Station opened it had only two platforms set against the outer walls. Passengers would enter the building via the booking hall on the western side and pass through to the departures platform, while the arriving trains pulled up on the opposite side of the station where travellers would find a waiting cab ready to take them to their destination. The central area between the two platforms was occupied by fourteen carriage 'roads' or sidings with inter-connecting turntables, and accordingly there was no concourse area as such at the end of the station. There was a sharp rise in railway usage during the second half of the nineteenth century, not least because the Midland Railway began running trains into King's Cross from 1858 and continued doing so until the construction of its own station, St Pancras. Consequently, King's Cross underwent several changes, mostly aimed at increasing capacity. Within the main station an additional arrivals platform was added in 1862, but it wasn't until 1893 that two further platforms were built down the middle of the station, necessitating the construction of the linking iron footbridge.

Externally there were far greater changes. The Metropolitan Railway opened in October 1863 with its own station, known as King's Cross Metropolitan (to the east of the main station and later to become King's Cross Thameslink). The Metropolitan 'Widened Lines' – a stretch of track with two extra lines – was linked to the Great Northern by two new underground connections. For local southbound trains heading towards Farringdon Street a single-line tunnel disappeared under York Road and these trains were served by York Road Platform, which opened in 1865 on the eastern side near the Gas Works Tunnel. Northbound trains from the Widened Lines emerged on the western side of the main station via a steep curving tunnel which passed under the Great Northern Hotel and hence was known as the Hotel Curve or more derisively by the railwaymen as the 'Drain'. In 1875 King's Cross (Local) was opened in an annexe attached to the main station on the western side at its front corner. The King's Cross (Suburban) station opened in 1878 on the Hotel Curve.

All this increase in traffic put enormous strain on the constricted 'throat', the short stretch of track funnelling into the Gas Works Tunnel. The situation was exacerbated by a rigid adherence to arrivals and departures sides and the resulting constant movement of locomotives. To alleviate the congestion, additional bores were created in 1878 and 1892.

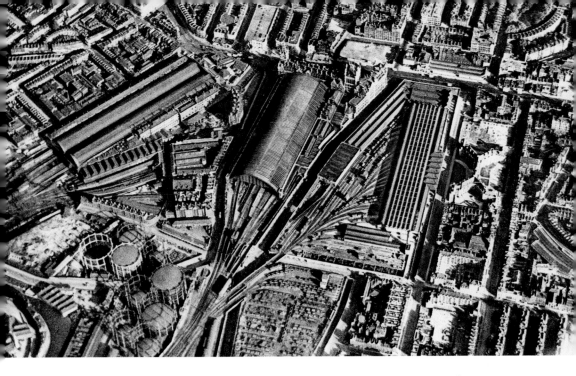

Aerial views of King's Cross and St Pancras, from the north and north-east. In the 1930s image King's Cross is to the left, the big roof of St Pancras in the centre and the Midland Railway Goods Yard to its right. The second picture was taken during the recent redevelopment – note the solitary gas holder, now gone. (*NetworkRail*)

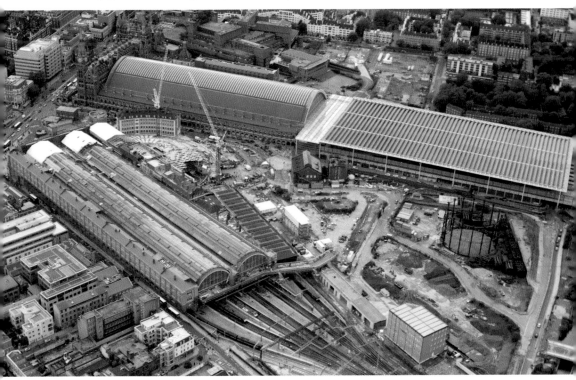

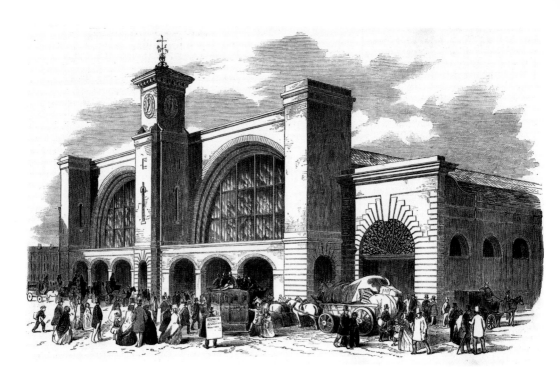

A bold front for the new station

The façade of Lewis Cubbitt's station, shown in an *Illustrated London News* engraving published shortly after its opening in 1852. The twin lunettes reflect and reveal the roofs within. On the right is the covered cab road beside Maiden Lane (York Way). It was later extended upwards as shown below.

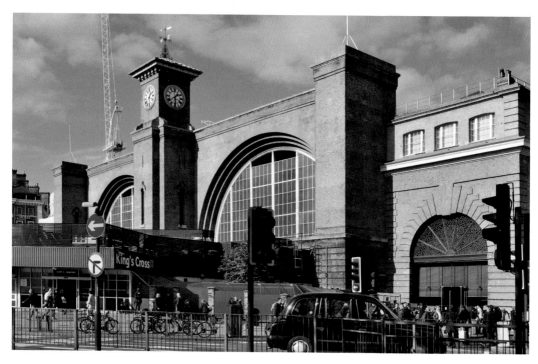

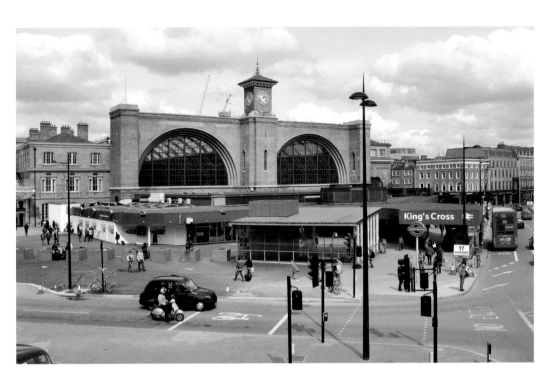

King's Cross seen from the St Pancras forecourt

The recent restoration has seen the lunettes re-glazed and they now reveal the roof structure within. As can be seen in the 1890s photo below, the area to the front of the station became cluttered with a number of structures including a wrought iron awning. Euston Road, leading into Pentonville Road, is on the right.

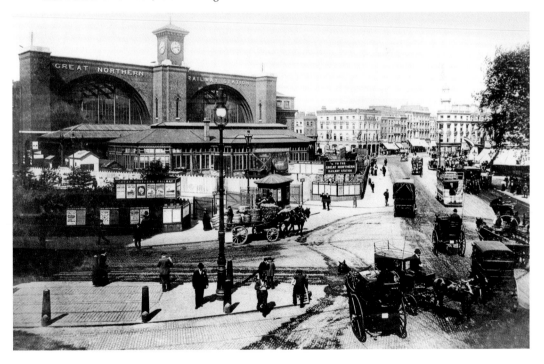

NEW ROOF OF PASSENGER STATION, GREAT NORTHERN RAILWAY, KING'S CROSS.

MR. RICHARD JOHNSON, M. INST. C.E., ENGINEER-IN-CHIEF.

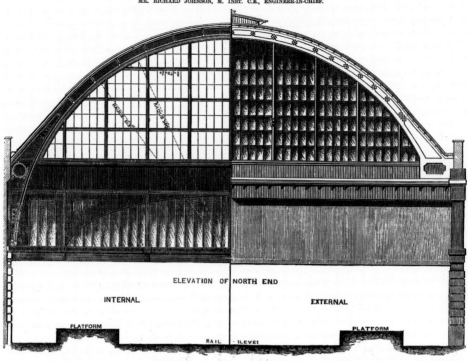

ELEVATION OF NORTH END

INTERNAL

EXTERNAL

PLATFORM

PLATFORM

RAIL LEVEL

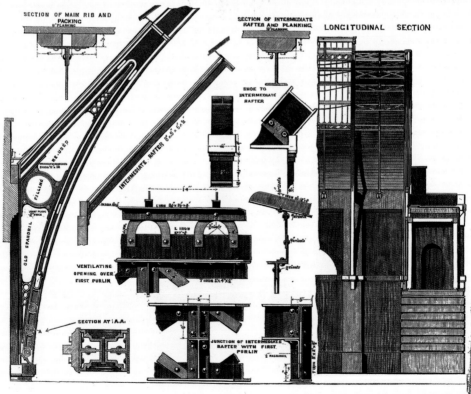

SECTION OF MAIN RIB AND PACKING

SECTION OF INTERMEDIATE RAFTER AND PLANKING

LONGITUDINAL SECTION

SHOE TO INTERMEDIATE RAFTER

INTERMEDIATE RAFTER

FILLING

OLD SPANDRIL

VENTILATING OPENING OVER FIRST PURLIN

SECTION AT A.A.

JUNCTION OF INTERMEDIATE RAFTER WITH FIRST PURLIN

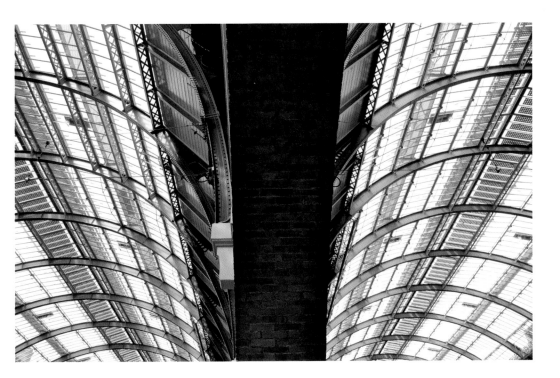

A new roof

By the 1860s the original laminated timber ribs supporting the roof were starting to deteriorate and they were replaced by iron ribs as shown in this 1870 illustration from *The Engineer*, opposite. The more recent upgrade has seen the installation of new glazing panels to bring the light pouring back into the old station.

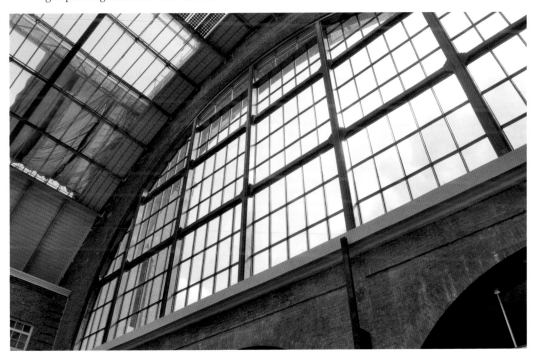

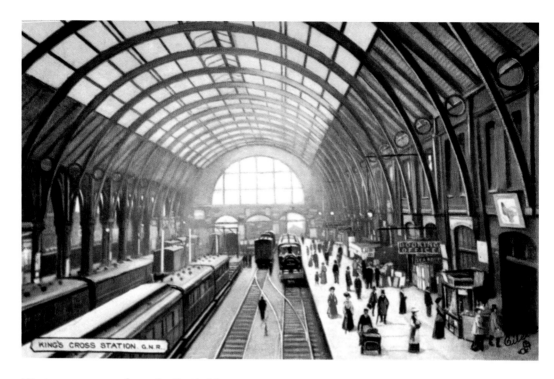

Western span seen from the footbridge

This postcard view from the GNR's heydays looks towards the town end of the station. The departures platform is on the right with the entrance from the west side of the building through the booking office. In the 2012 photograph the platform has been de-cluttered, but the all-grey trains make it feel very monochromatic.

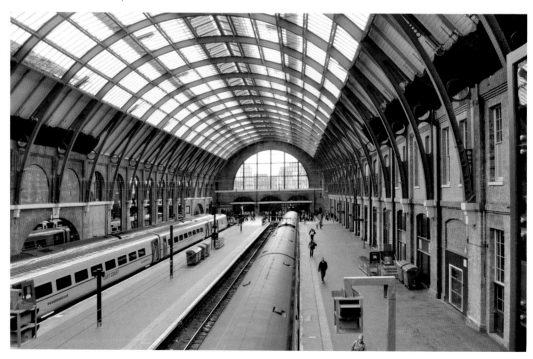

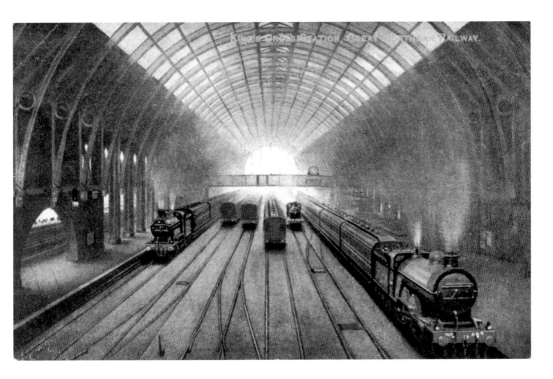

The Eastern span

The eastern side of the station, facing towards the country end, with the arrivals platform on the right. In the distance is the iron footbridge with clock, and in the lower photograph the new footbridge is in place although the restoration of the roof is still in progress.

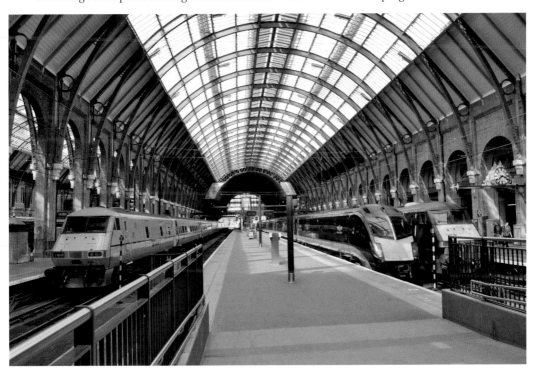

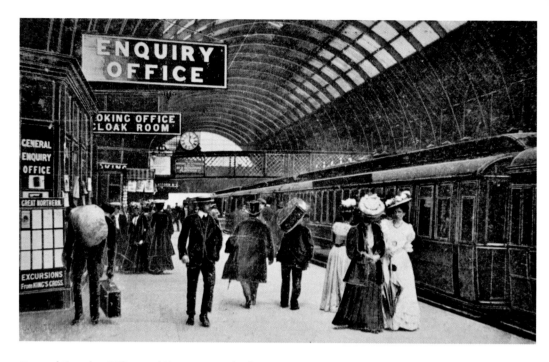

General Enquiry Office and Departures Platform
Close up view of the GNR Enquiries Office at the turn of the century, with the Booking Office and Cloak Room off to the left. Photographed below in 2010 during the renovation, with a Grand Central train about to depart for the north-east. Grand Central began operating out of King's Cross in 2007.

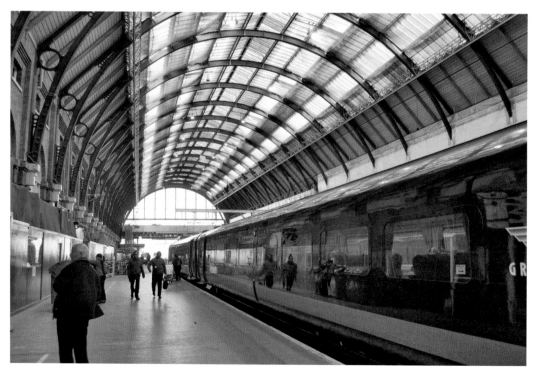

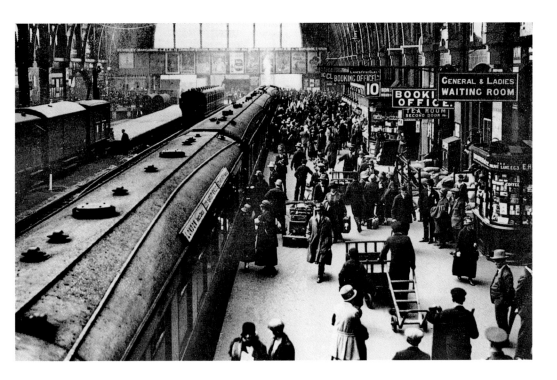

Platforms

A platform crowded with travellers, railway porters and several kiosks and bookstalls, from the early LNER days. Note the row of advertising hoardings beneath the lunette window. Below, an East Coast ex-BR Class 91 electric loco waiting beside a Grand Central Class 180 Adelante diesel multiple unit.

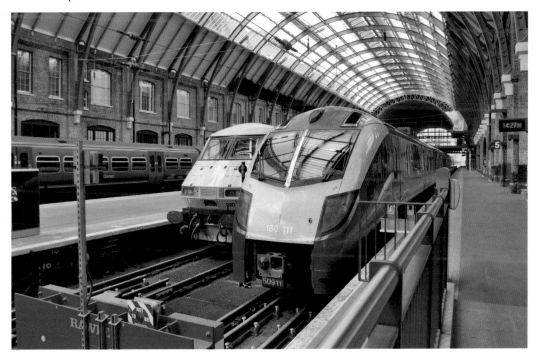

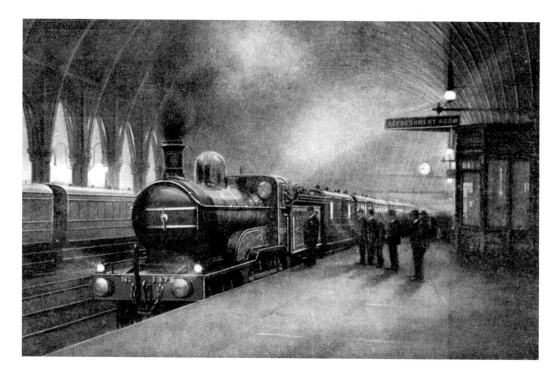

Night and day

'King's Cross station by night' – an atmospheric postcard view from *c.* 1900. Below, this loco, named *James Herriot* after the famous Yorkshire vet, is a Grand Central Class 180, photographed in the autumn of 2010 on Platform 8 with evidence of the station refurbishment work in the background.

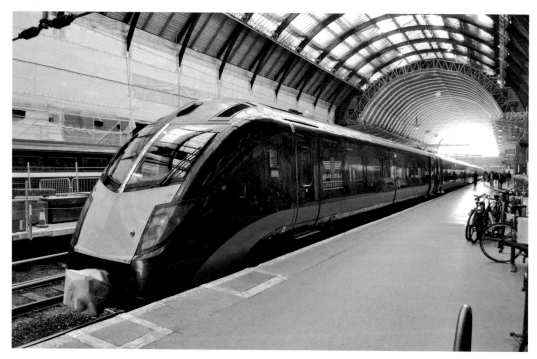

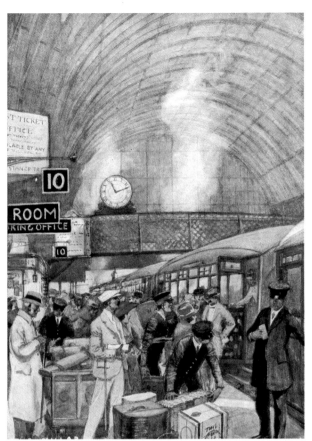

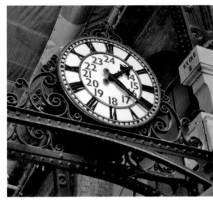

The 1893 Handyside footbridge and clock

A fine period illustration of the Departures Platform with iron footbridge and clock in the background. The footbridge was dismantled in 2009 and donated to the Mid Hants Railway. This is the GNR station clock on Platform 1.

Below, the new modern footbridge with access via escalators and lifts.

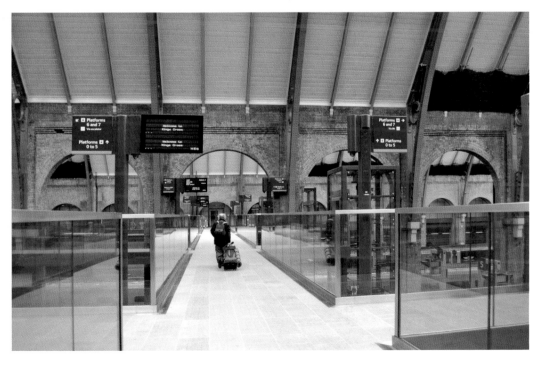

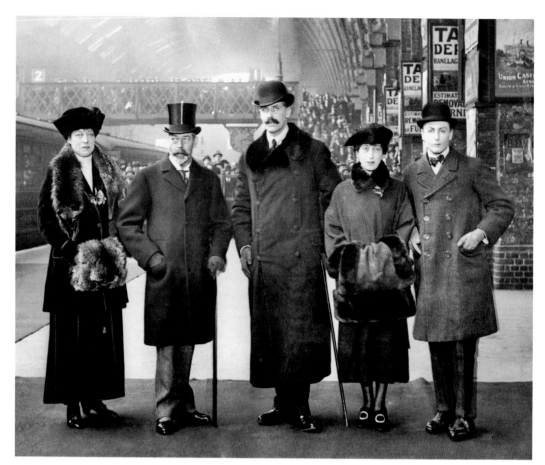

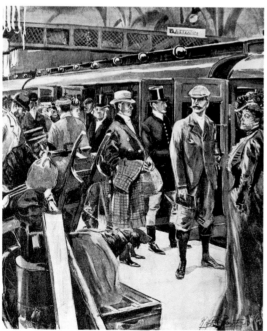

Going North

King's Cross welcomed some distinguished travellers in 1922 – Princess Victoria, King George V, the King and Queen of Norway and Prince Olaf. In the nineteenth century the artist George Earl had painted a scene of fashionable passengers about to depart with their dogs and guns on the way to Scotland for the start of the shooting season. This illustration, left, is from a 1900 edition of *The Graphic* and shows 'The end of the London Season – the exodus to the North'.

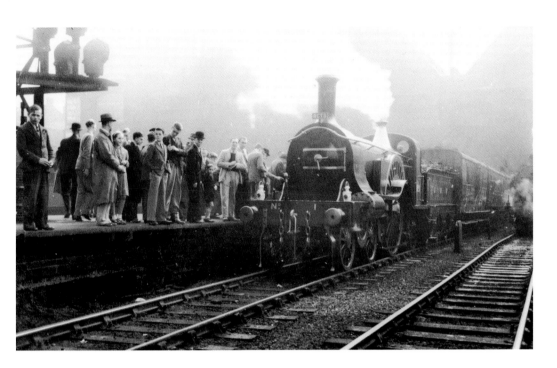

King's Cross departures

An interesting photo of the GNR Stirling 4-2-2 No. 1 at King's Cross during the 1952 centenary celebrations. Designed by Patrick Stirling, No. 1 is now part of the National Railway Museum's collection. The modern photo of this part of the station was taken in 2010 while renovation work was in progress.

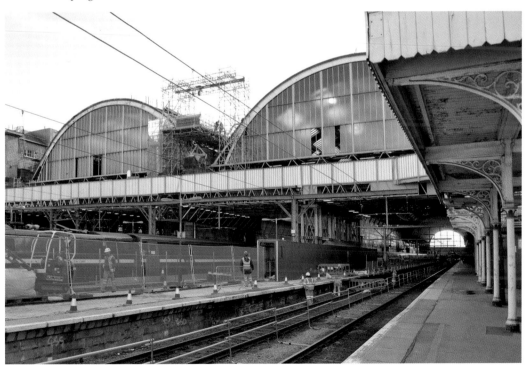

20th Century King's Cross

The Railways Act of 1921 brought Britain's independent railways together within the 'Big Four' regional companies; the Great Western Railway (GWR), the London & North Eastern Railway (LNER), the Southern Railway (SR) and the London Midland & Scottish Railway (LMS). The LNER was the second biggest after the LMS, and in addition to the Great Northern Railway its constituent companies included the Great Eastern Railway, the Great Central Railway, the Great North of Scotland Railway and the North Eastern Railway. When the Act came into effect on 1 January 1923 the LNER inherited several London stations including Liverpool Street and Marylebone as well as King's Cross, which became its main London terminus.

The principal route for the LNER was the East Coast Main Line from King's Cross to Edinburgh via York and Newcastle upon Tyne, and beyond Edinburgh up to Aberdeen and Inverness. This was in direct competition with the LMS West Coast Main Line and the inter-war years saw a period of intense rivalry as both companies strived to set new speed records with some of the finest steam locomotives ever seen. It was also the golden age of the famous named train services such as the Flying Scotsman, Night Scotsman and Yorkshire Pullman.

At King's Cross there had been little physical change since the end of the nineteenth century until the arrival of the LNER. The two over-bridges between the station and Gas Works Tunnel had been removed by 1921 and replaced by the Goods Way road. In 1923 the small loco yard between the suburban and local stations was moved further down to the west side of the lines entering Gas Works Tunnel. By 1924 a second departure platform was finally added within the station (the suburban station also got an additional island platform) and then in 1934 a short platform was abolished so another could be lengthened. 1932 saw major upgrades to the signalling with the introduction of colour lights and electrically worked points. And that was about it until the post-war nationalisation and the British Railways years.

Even then the major changes did not come until the 1970s with the electrification of suburban services and the introduction of the InterCity 125 High Speed Trains. The track layout was simplified and this included closing one of the three Gas Works tunnels, and both the York Road and Suburban platforms closed in 1977. At the other end of the station the accumulation of kiosks and buildings in front of Cubbitt's façade was swept away and replaced by a supposedly temporary single-storey canopy to house the Booking Office and Travel Centre.

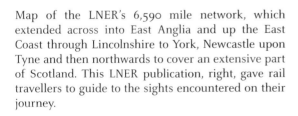

LONDON & NORTH EASTERN RAILWAY

East Coast
Route
Shortest and
Quickest
between
England and
Scotland.

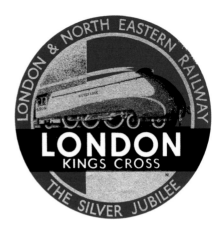

Luggage Label for LNER's flagship Silver Jubilee streamliner trains – see page 30.

Map of the LNER's 6,590 mile network, which extended across into East Anglia and up the East Coast through Lincolnshire to York, Newcastle upon Tyne and then northwards to cover an extensive part of Scotland. This LNER publication, right, gave rail travellers to guide to the sights encountered on their journey.

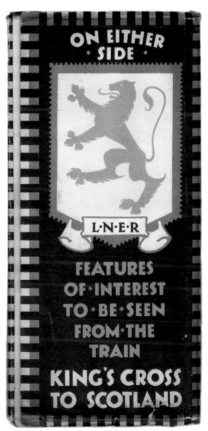

ON EITHER
· SIDE ·

L·N·E·R

FEATURES
OF·INTEREST
TO·BE·SEEN
FROM·THE
TRAIN

KING'S CROSS
TO SCOTLAND

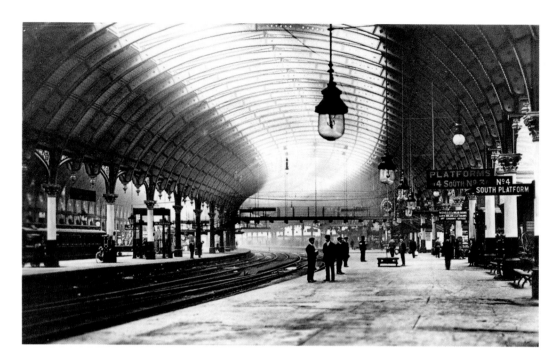

Destination York

The station at York lies approximately 188 miles north of King's Cross and halfway on the East Coast Main Line to Edinburgh. The present station was opened in 1887 by the North Eastern Railway and at that time it was the largest in the world. The 800-foot iron roof is all the more impressive as it was built on a curve. York was also a major site for the manufacture and maintenance of railway rolling stock.

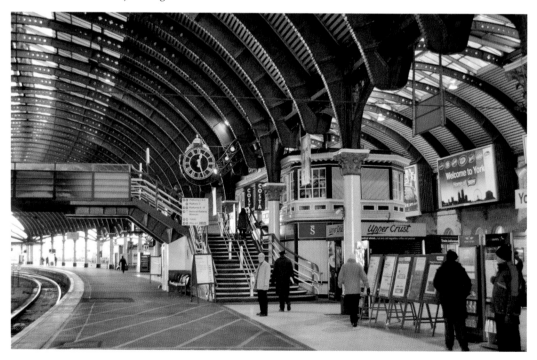

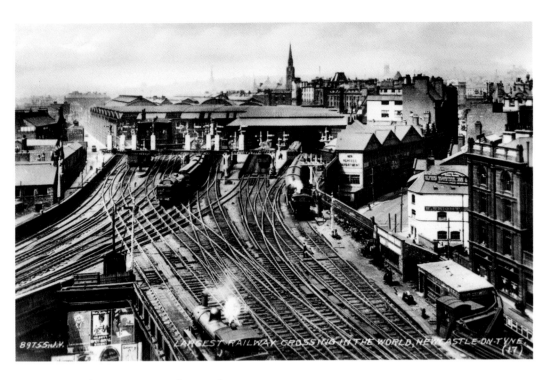

Newcastle upon Tyne and Waverley

Newcastle, above, splits the leg between York and Edinburgh into two. It opened in 1850 for the York, Newcastle & Berwick Railway and the Newcastle & Carlisle Railway, which later merged with other companies to form the North Eastern Railway. Waverley is the main station for Edinburgh and the second largest in the UK.

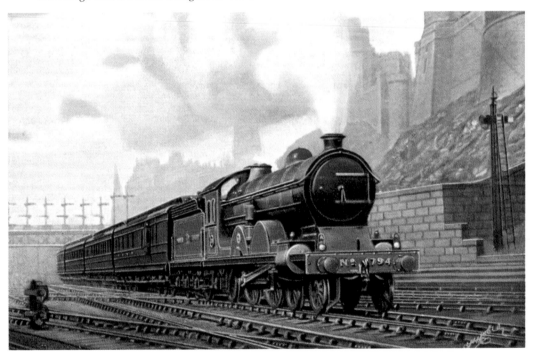

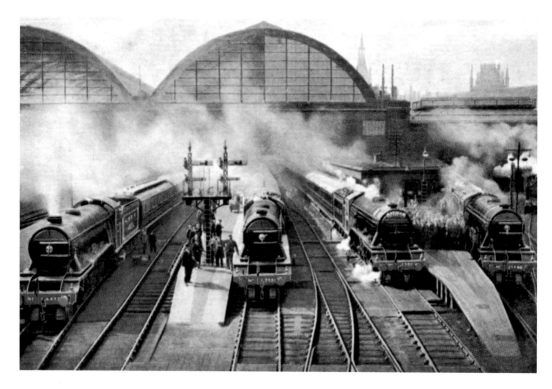

'Morning rush-hour from King's Cross to the North'
'10.15 a.m. Leeds Express, 10.05 Scotch Express, 10.00 a.m. Non-stop Flying Scotsman, 10.20 a.m. Peterborough.' Surely the golden age of King's Cross. In comparison the modern station seen from Goods Way is a jungle of gantries, not helped by the scaffolding covering the end of the train sheds.

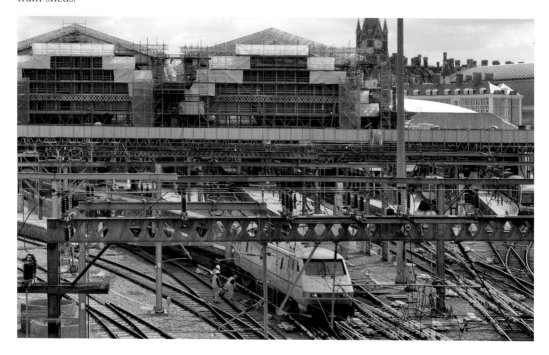

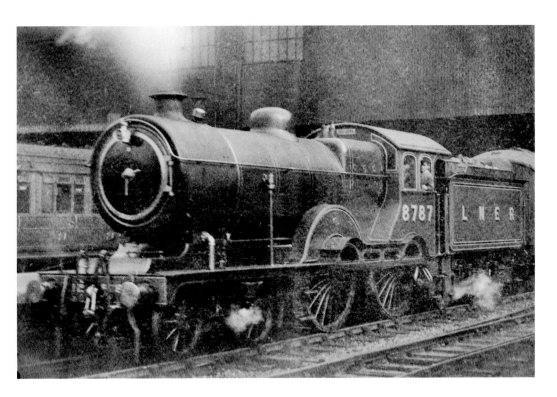

Getting away

The LNER's rebuilt D16/3 class *Claud Hamilton* No. 8787 leaving King's Cross. Three classes of the former Great Eastern Railway locomotives were nicknamed as the Clauds or Super Clauds after the first, *Claud Hamilton* No. 1900, which took to the tracks in the year 1900. The design is credited to James Holden. In the lower image the Granary can be seen in the distance beyond the loco. (*CMcC*)

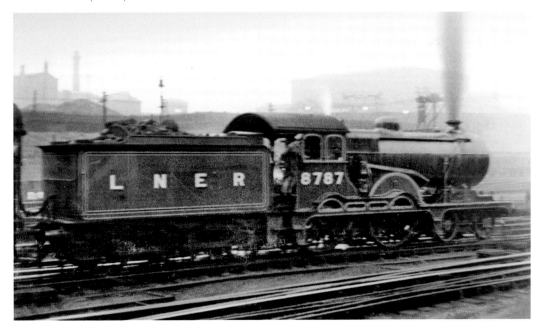

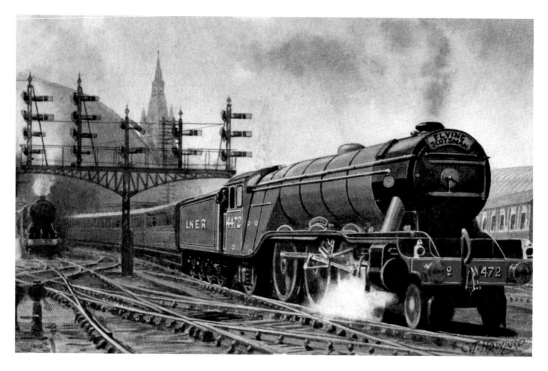

The Flying Scotsman

No. 4774, *Flying Scotsman*, was a GNR Nigel Gresley-designed A1 when built at the Doncaster Works in 1923, later rebuilt as an LNER A3 Pacific in 1947. It is now preserved by the National Railway Museum. In the 2005 photograph, below, it is shown wearing a pair of German-style smoke deflectors. (*Michael J. Irlam*)

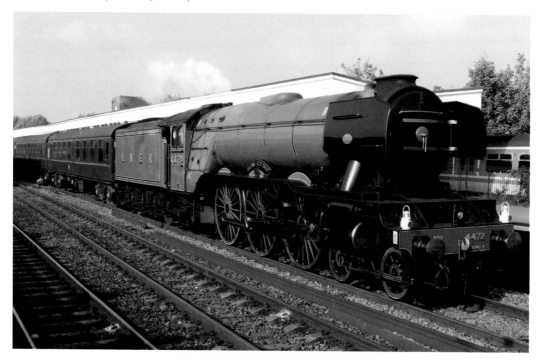

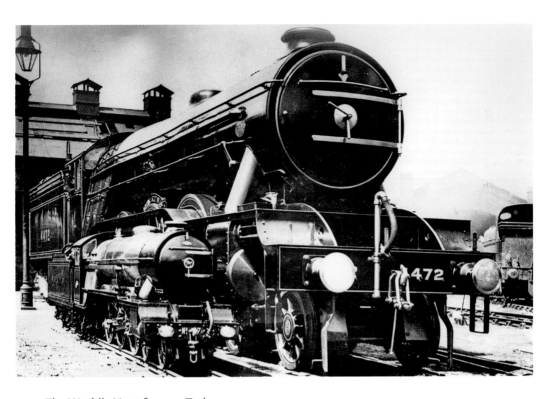

The World's Most famous Train

No. 4472 *Flying Scotsman* became something of a celebrity. It is shown in the King's Cross yard with a miniature working copy for the Romney, Hythe & Dymchurch Railway, *c.* 1924. It is also featured in the LNER publication from 1925, and in this contemporary illustration of a departure from King's Cross with a 'night express for the north'.

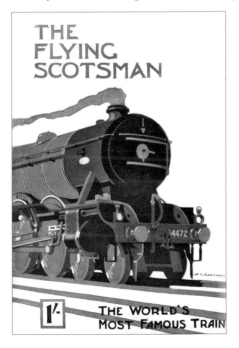

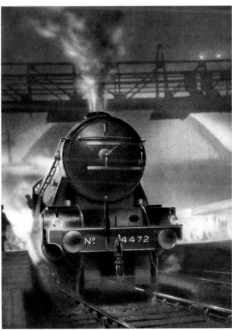

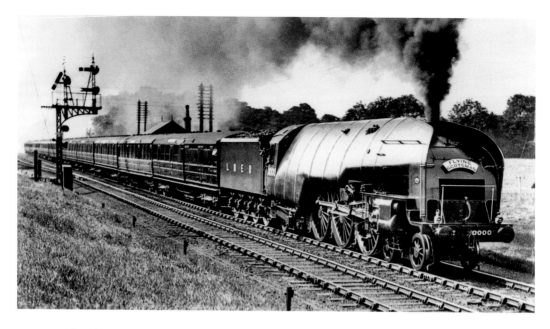

No. 10000 'Hush-Hush'

This was an experimental W1 class locomotive fitted with a high-pressure water tube boiler. Designed by Gresley, it was built at the LNER's Darlington Works in 1929. Although based on a Pacific 4-6-2 chassis it had an extra axle to accommodate the greater length, resulting in a unique 4-6-4 configuration.

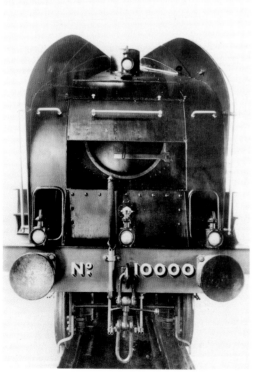

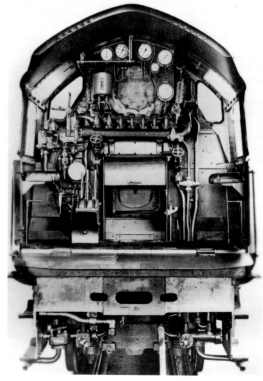

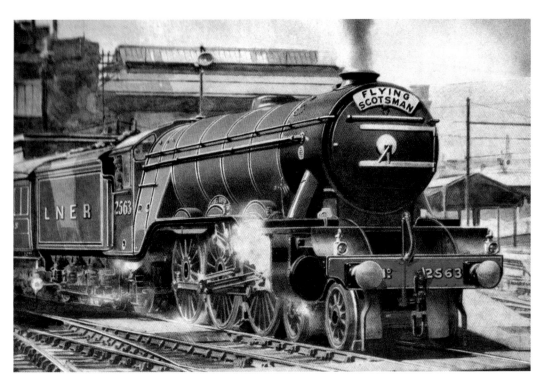

Day and night
No. 2563 *William Whitelaw*, an A1/A3 Pacific named after the LNER's first chairman, is shown here departing from King's Cross with the Local/Suburban station in the background. Below, night departures seen from Goods Way: 2548 *Galtee More* and 4474 *Victor Wild* hauling the Night Scotsman. (*CMcC*)

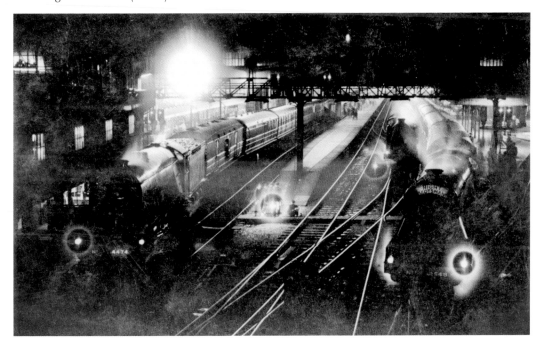

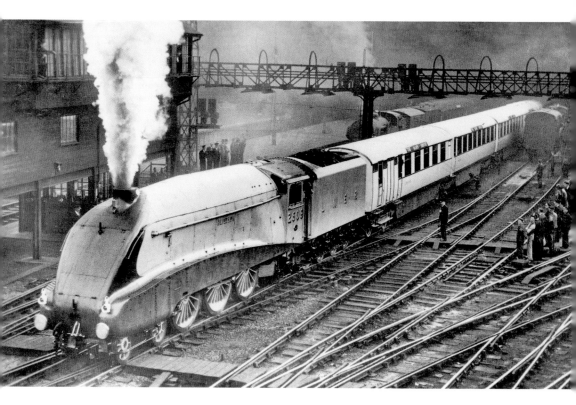

Silver Jubilee and *Silver Link*

29 September 1935: The year of King George V's silver jubilee, and the A4 class *Silver Link* 2509 is shown departing from King's Cross hauling the inaugural Silver Jubilee express to Newcastle. This was the first fully streamlined train and even the gaps between the coaches were smoothed over with rubber sheeting. Sustaining an average speed of 100 mph at times, the *Silver Link* peaked with a new record of 112 mph, provoking a speed war with the rival LMS. *Silver Link* was the first A4 to emerge from the Doncaster Works and a further three A4 locos were built for the Silver Jubilee service. Below, *Silver Link* shown in a classic cutaway from the *Eagle* comic in 1960. No. 2509 remained in service until 1963, when it handed over to the Deltics.

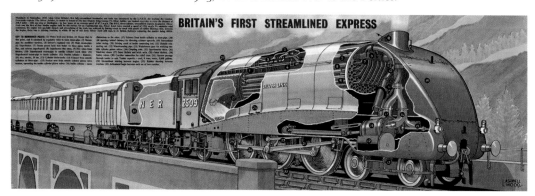

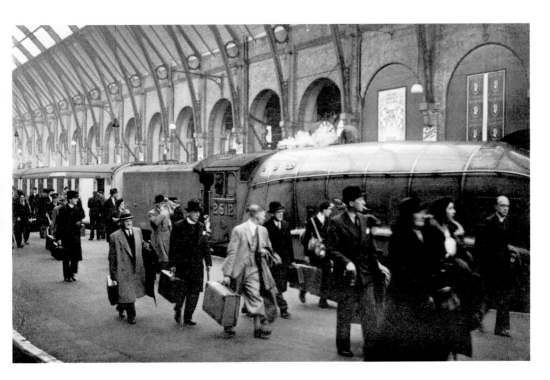

Silver Fox

The *Silver Fox* 2512 shortly after arriving at King's Cross. This was the fourth of the A4 Pacifics built for the Silver Jubilee service. You can just make out part of the fox emblem on the side, between the porter and the man smoking. (*CmcC*) Below, today's arrivals, 180112 for Grand Central and 82223 for East Coast.

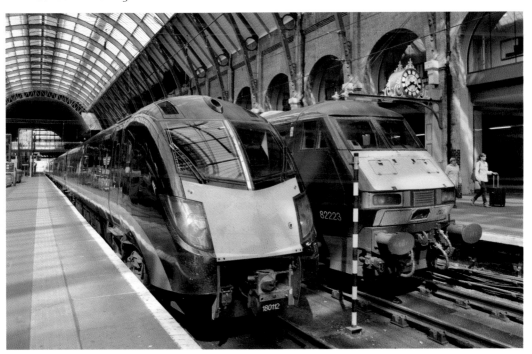

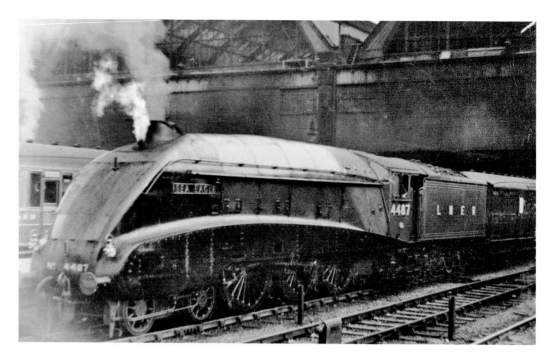

Sea Eagle and Mallard

No. 4487 *Sea Eagle* departing from King's Cross. Following the initial four A4s the LNER built a further thirty-one for express services, introduced in 1936–37. Many were named after birds, although the *Sea Eagle* was changed to *Walter K. Whigham* in 1947. *Mallard* famously set an absolute speed record of 126 mph in 1938.

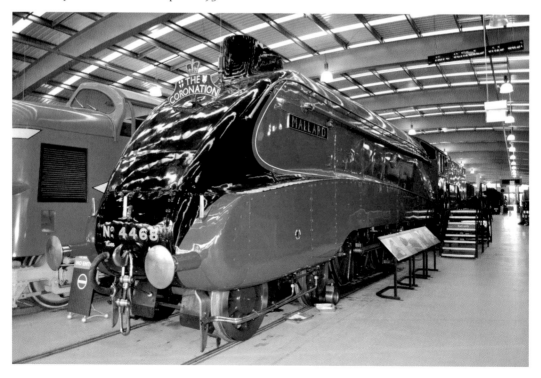

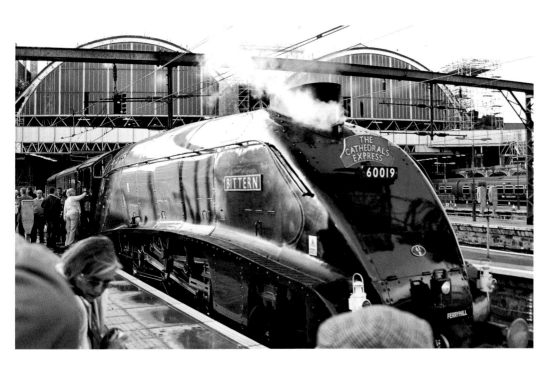

Preserved A4s

Six of the A4s have been preserved, four of them in the UK – *Bittern, Mallard, Union of South Africa* and *Sir Nigel Gresley*. *Bittern*, with British Railways number 60019 (previously 4464 under the LNER), is shown hauling the Silver Jubilee 75th anniversary train at King's Cross in 2010. (*Steel City Ady*) Below, *Sir Nigel Gresley* No. 60007 (was 4498) at Watlington Station, 2010. (*Lewis Collard*)

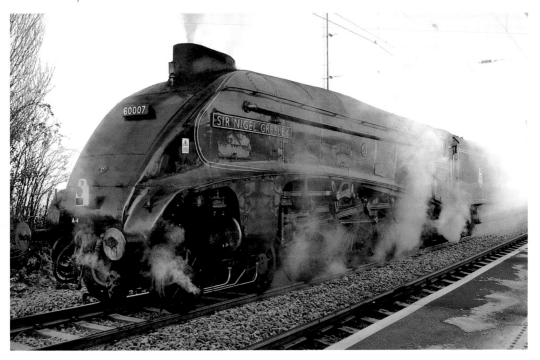

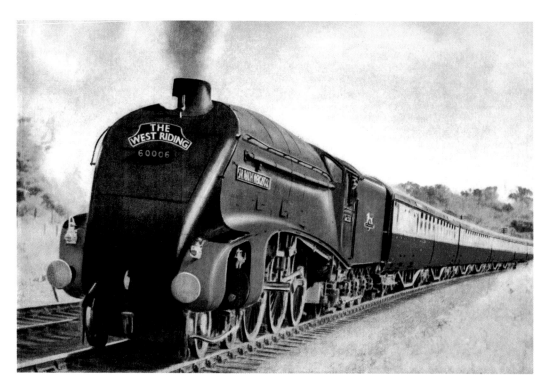

True blue

Two ex-LNER locos sporting the British Railways lion and hauling the red and cream coaches, but still resplendent in black and blue. Above, 60006 *Sir Ralph Wedgwood*, previously 4466 *Herring Gull* (renamed in 1947). Below, 60036 *Colombo* A3 class, previously LNER No. 2501.

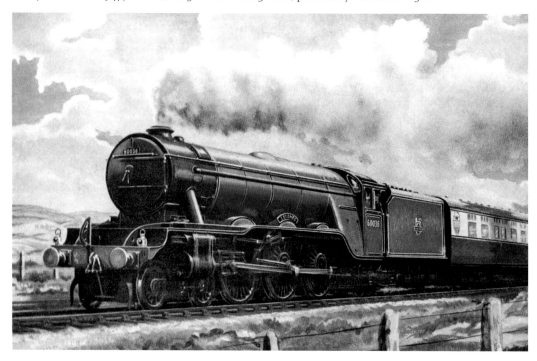

North-east connections

60010 *The Dominion of Canada*, depicted on the cover of a 1956 edition of *Meccano Magazine* hauling The Norseman train out of King's Cross. This service ran from London to the Newcastle upon Tyne Commission Quay to connect with ships of the Bergen Line or Fred Olsen Line to Norway. Below, Darlington's fabulous brick *Mallard* was created in 1977 by artist David Mach. It took thirty-four brick-layers, labourers and apprentices twenty-one weeks to build the train using 18,500 bricks.

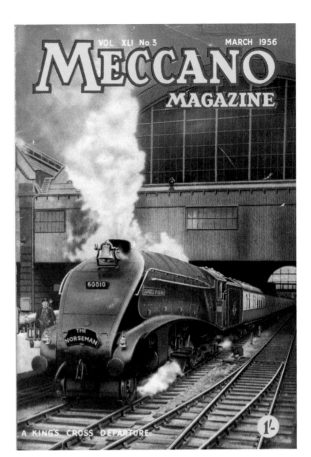

VOL. XLI No. 3   MARCH 1956

MECCANO
MAGAZINE

A KING'S CROSS DEPARTURE

1/-

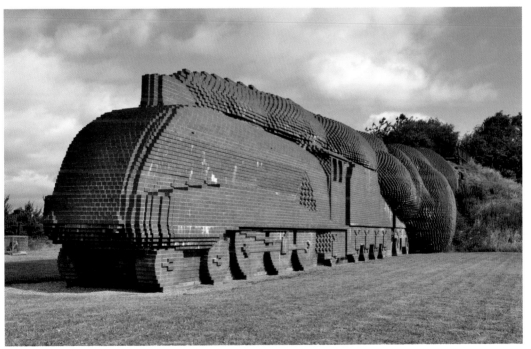

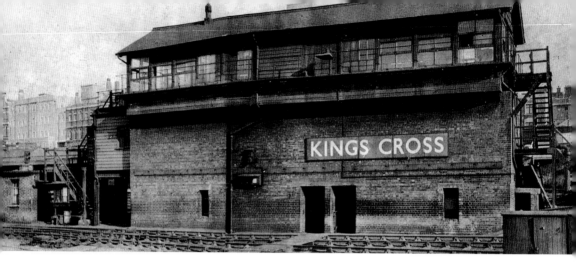

King's Cross Signal Box
Shown above *c.* 1960, and below in this illustration of No. 60537 *Bachelors Button,* a Peppercorn Class A2 which entered service in 1948. All save the first fifteen A2s were built for British Railways after nationalisation.

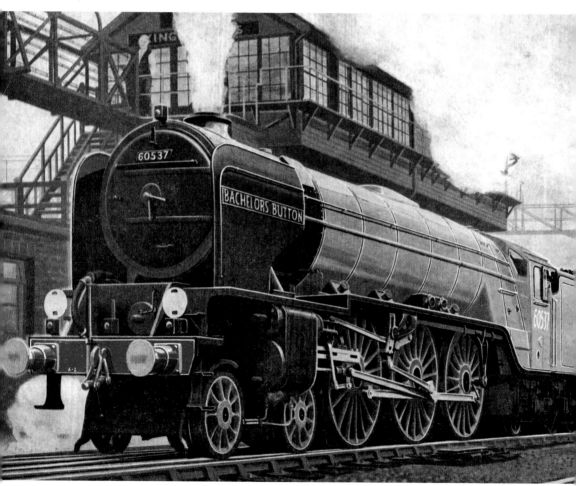

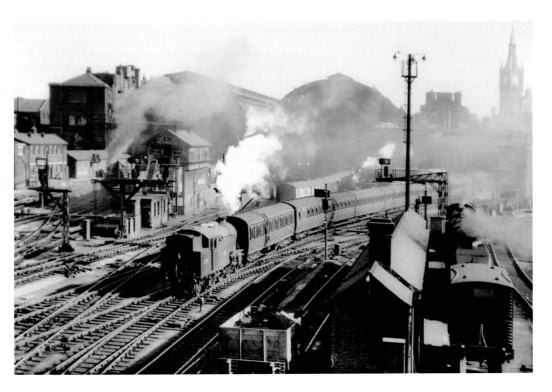

Signal Box and approach

A view from Goods Way in the 1950s showing the Signal Box in the thick of the action. The tank engine is 67784, a British Railways L1 class 2-6-4T which entered service in 1950 and was withdrawn in 1962. In the 2012 view the Signal Box has gone, as have the small buildings to the left and the small loco yard on the right.

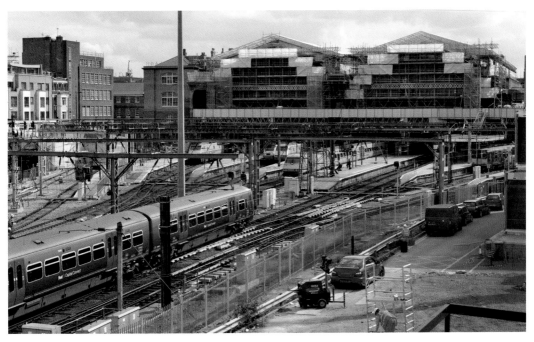

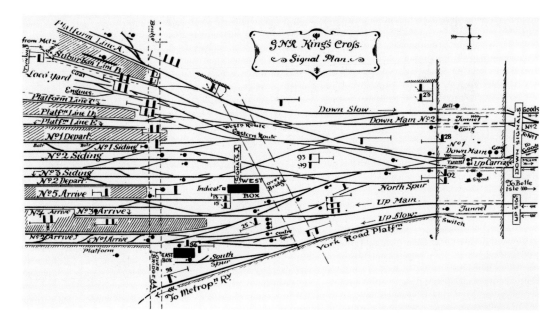

Clearing the throat

Station on the left: In the 1905 signal plan the Suburban Station is top left with Line B emerging from the 'Drain'. Beneath this are a Loco Yard and Platforms D and E of the Local Station. The main signal box is shown as West Box with an additional East Box by the south spur and line down to the Metropolitan on the eastern side. Below, before and after of the 1978 operation to prepare the station for the InterCity 125s. Most notably the Suburban platforms are gone, as are the sidings and diesel shed on the west side. The eastern bore of Gas Works Tunnel is no longer used and the York Road Platform and line to the Met have gone.

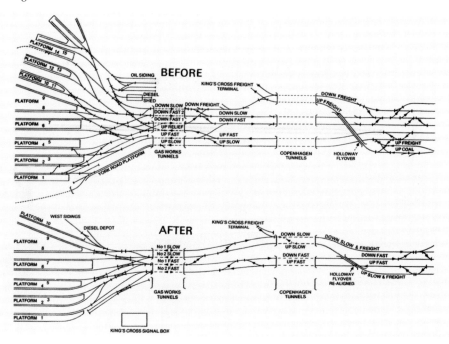

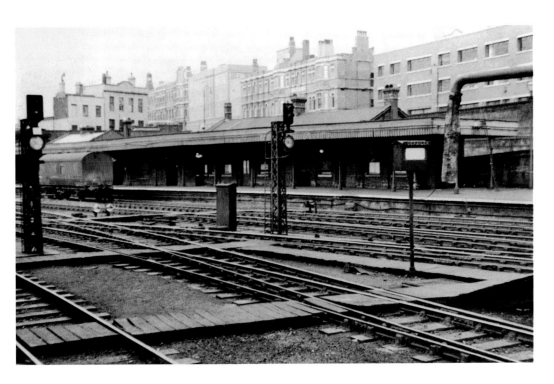

York Road Platform and Signal Box

Two views looking across to the York Road Platform on the eastern side of the lines with Gas Works Tunnel on the left. In the lower picture the new Signal Box, completed in 1977, has appeared at the far end of the York Road Platform. (*Colourrail*)

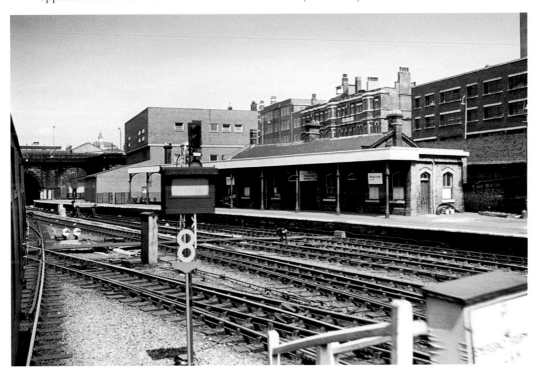

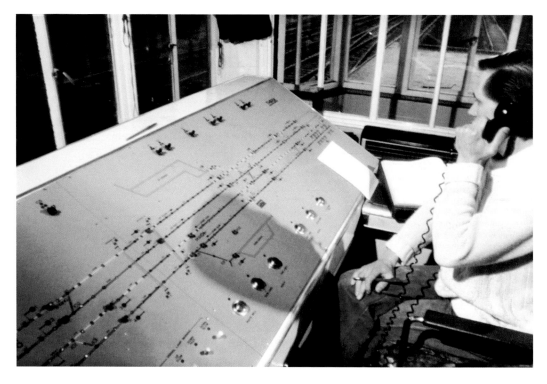

Signal boxes

Above, a British Rail publicity photograph from the 1970s showing a state-of-the-art electronic signal box on the East Coast Main Line. Below, a recent photo of the signalling floor of the refurbished King's Cross Signal Box, shown opposite. (*NetworkRail*)

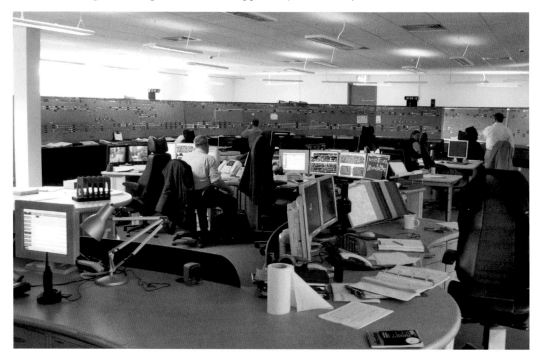

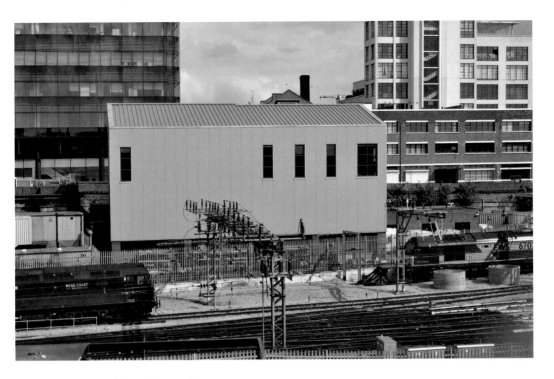

The eastern side of the station

The 1970s King's Cross Signal Box has been refurbished inside and out with this new facade. It stands at the northern end of the old York Road Platform (demolished). Below, the lesser known side of King's Cross Station on York Way. The lower floor was originally a cab road, but now houses the new Platform o.

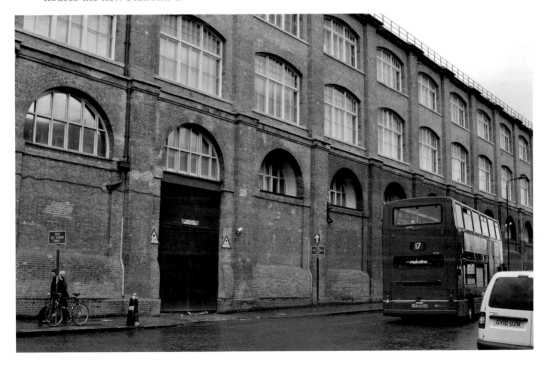

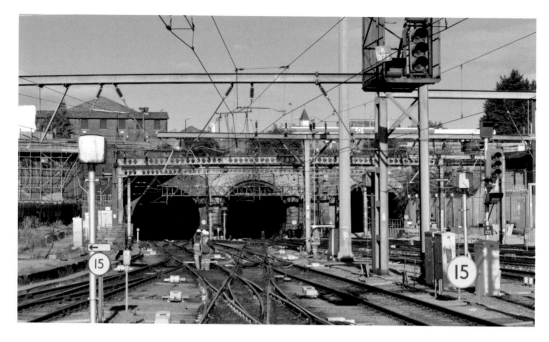

Gas Works Tunnel

The triple bores of the Gas Works Tunnel, which passes under the Regent's Canal. The one on the far right is no longer used by the trains. The Signal Box is off-frame to the right, and top left you can see some of the Goods Yard buildings. Below, harking back to the 1960s, a young train-spotter waits patiently at the end of York Road Platform with the portico of the Gas Work Tunnel to the left.

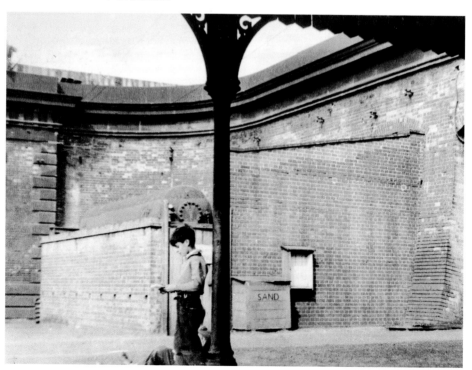

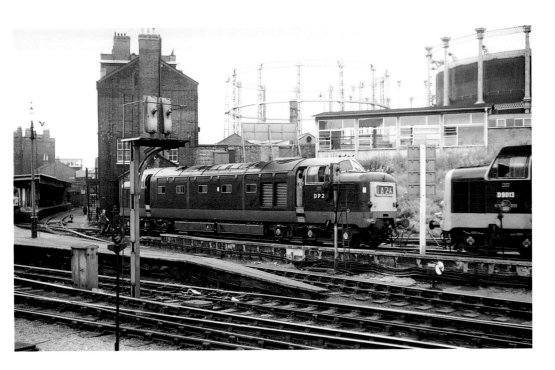

The western side

A superb photograph from 1969 with the Culross Buildings – built to house company workers – and to the left the Suburban Station platforms. This Deltic is either coming in or out of the Diesel Shed out of the frame on the right. (*Colourrail*) Detail of the old canopy at the end of Platform 8/9 and dividing wall.

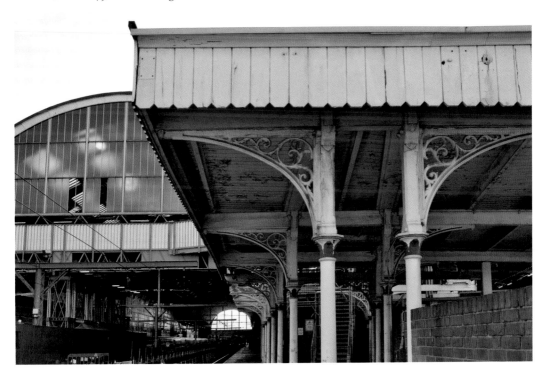

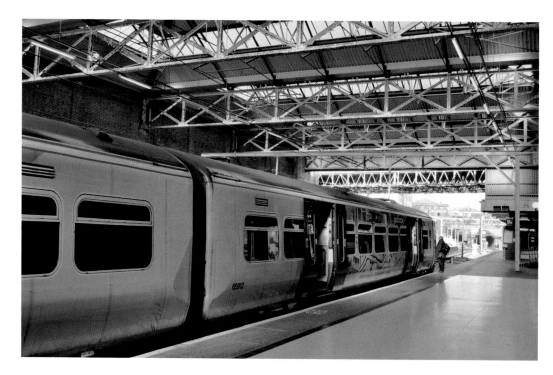

Platforms 9–11

The Local Station annexe, now Platforms 9–11 for suburban services. For a while Harry Potter's Platform 9¾ trolley was on the wall at the end of Platform 9, but this has been moved to the new concourse area – see page 83. A pair of Networker Express Class 365 EMUs for First Capital Connect, photographed in October 2010.

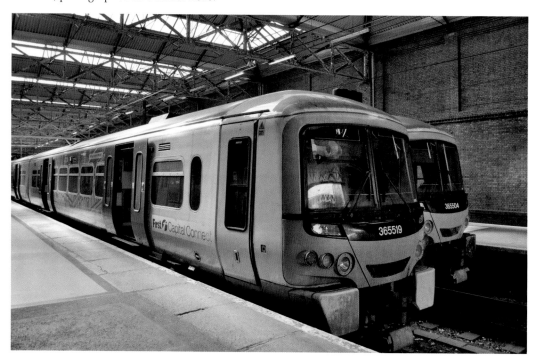

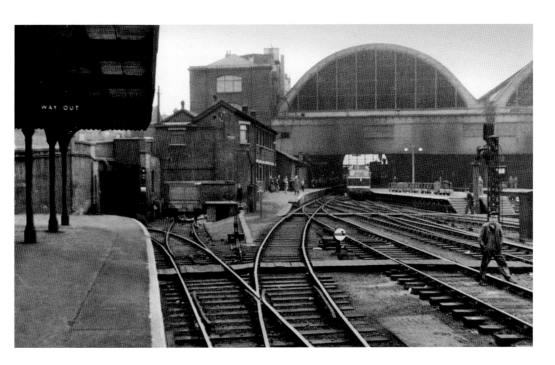

Platform 0

The newest platform at King's Cross is Platform 0, which occupies the former cab road on the east side. In the upper view, taken from York Road Platform *c.* 1964, the southbound tunnel to the Widened Lines is on the left and the buildings at the end of the short spur are to be demolished to provide rail access to the new platform.

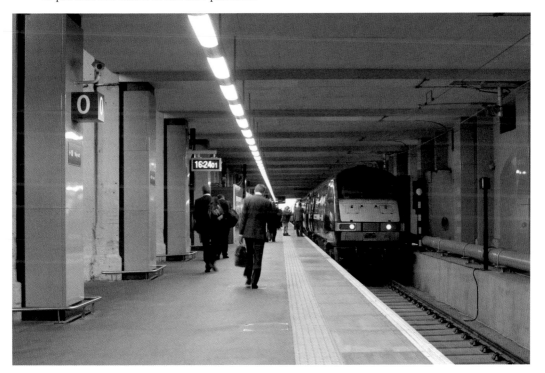

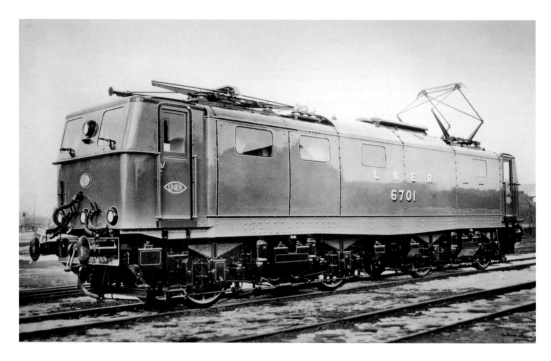

Farewell to steam

No. 6701 is the prototype for the LNER's EM1 Bo-Bo (four wheel bogie) class of electric locomotive. It was built at Doncaster in 1940, but the production versions did not appear until after the post-war nationalisation. No. 26020 is preserved at the National Railway Museum in its original British Railways black.

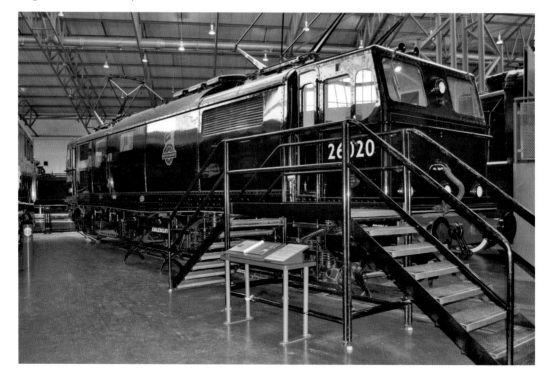

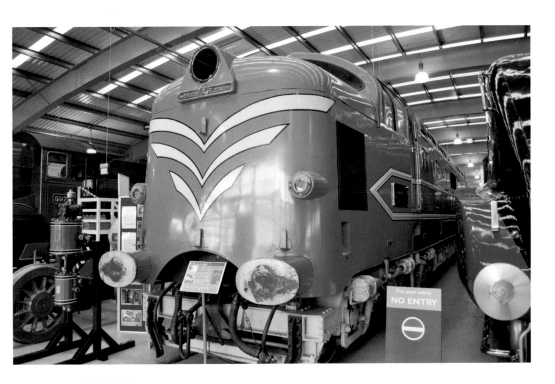

Dawn of the Deltics

DP1, the prototype for the 3300hp English Electric Co-Co's which became known as the Deltics. On display at the NRM Shildon and finished in powder blue, it has a positively American feel with high cab and central lamp. British Rail ordered twenty-two of the Class 55 Deltics. No. 55002, *The Kings Own Yorkshire Light Infantry*, is shown in early two-tone green livery at King's Cross. (*Phil Sangwell*)

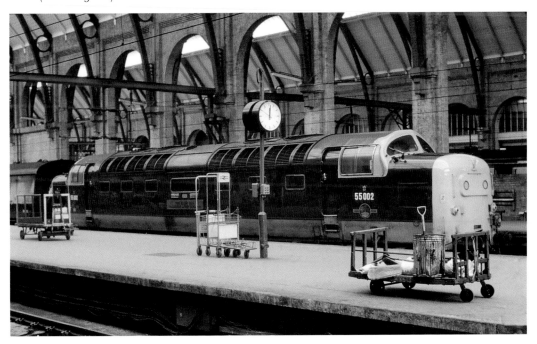

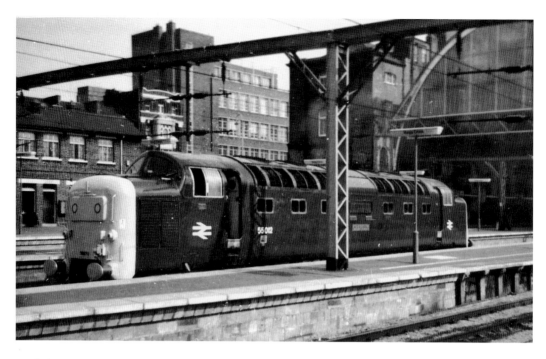

English Electric Deltic and General Electric Class 91

The Deltics hauled the Flying Scotsman throughout the 1960s and 1970s, achieving record times on the East Coast run. This is 55012 *Creppello* at King's Cross; it was withdrawn in 1981. The same view looking back at the north-east corner of the station into York Way in 2012 with an East Coast former British Rail Class 91.

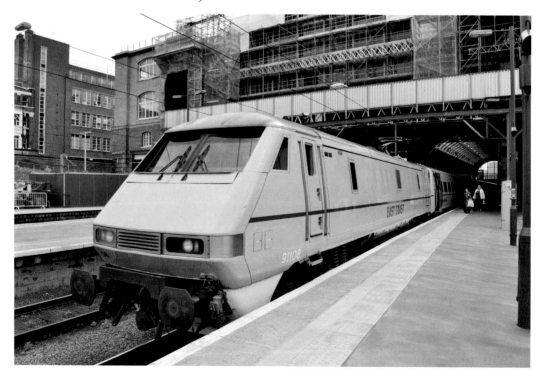

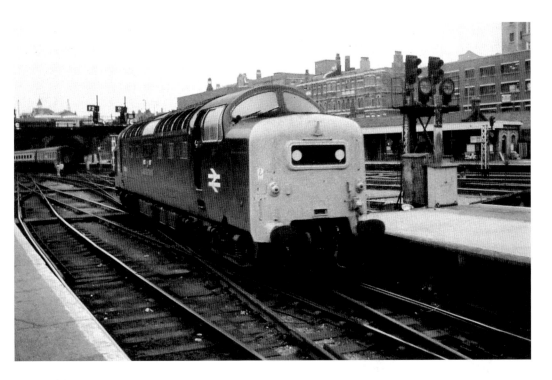

Deltics

Deltic at King's Cross in 1976, with York Road Platform in the background. (*Dave John*) Below, 55002 *The Kings Own Yorkshire Light Infantry* again – see p47 – this time in blue and yellow in the workshop at the National Railway Museum in York, photographed in late 2010.

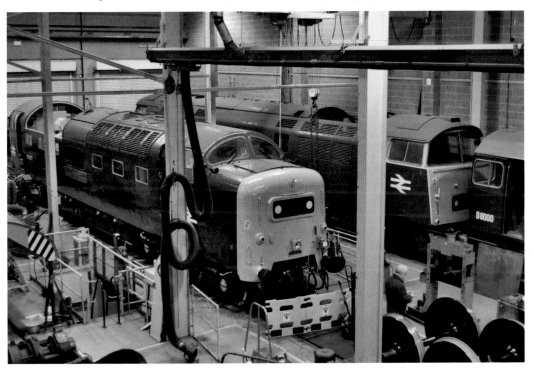

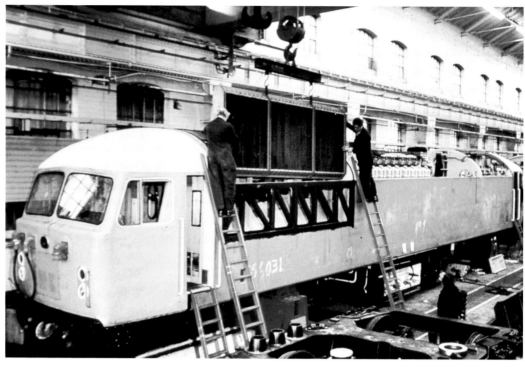

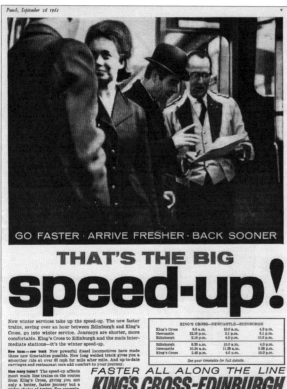

Punch, September 26 1962

GO FASTER · ARRIVE FRESHER · BACK SOONER

THAT'S THE BIG
speed-up!

Now winter services take up the speed-up. The new faster trains, saving over an hour between Edinburgh and King's Cross, go into winter service. Journeys are shorter, more comfortable. King's Cross to Edinburgh and the main intermediate stations—It's the winter speed-up.

New locos — new track New powerful diesel locomotives have made these new timetables possible. New long welded track gives you a smoother ride at over 90 mph for mile after mile. And up-to-date carriages and restaurant cars add comfort to your journey.

How many trains? The speed-up affects most main line trains on the routes from King's Cross, giving you not only a better, faster journey but a wider choice of trains. For example, three trains each way make the daily journey between London and Edinburgh in less than 6 hrs. 20 mins.

KING'S CROSS—NEWCASTLE—EDINBURGH		
King's Cross	6.0 a.m.	10.0 a.m.	4.0 p.m.
Newcastle	12.16 p.m.	3.1 p.m.	8.1 p.m.
Edinburgh	2.19 p.m.	4.0 p.m.	10.0 p.m.
Edinburgh	8.30 a.m.	10.0 a.m.	4.0 p.m.
Newcastle	10.34 a.m.	11.58 a.m.	5.58 p.m.
King's Cross	2.45 p.m.	4.0 p.m.	10.0 p.m.

See your timetable for full details.

FASTER ALL ALONG THE LINE
KING'S CROSS-EDINBURGH
SHEFFIELD · LEEDS · NEWCASTLE   BRITISH RAILWAYS

Diesel power

Above, British Rail publicity photograph of 56031, a Class 56 diesel nearing completion at the Doncaster Works. These were designed for heavy freight work and introduced from 1976 onwards. Left, this British Railways advert from 1962 promotes the 'Big Speed-up' with the new, shorter journey times achieved by the Deltics: 'New powerful diesel locomotives have made these new timetables possible. Three trains each way make the daily journey from London to Edinburgh in less than 6 hrs 20 mins.'

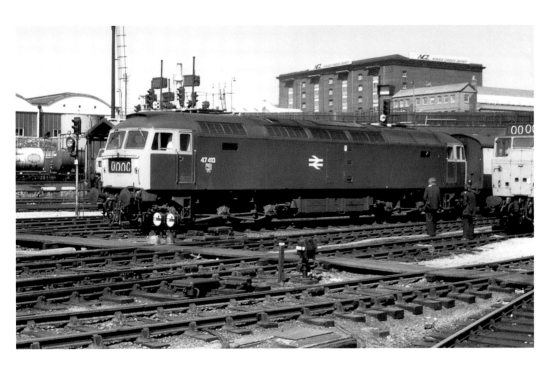

Class 47 diesel-electrics

In the 1960s 512 Class 47s were built at Crewe and Loughborough for use on passenger and freight services. Above, 47413 arriving at King's Cross with an InterCity express in May 1976. Note the Granary building in the distance (compare this scene with the one on p25). Below, another King's Cross Class 47, this time 47408 heading off for servicing at Finsbury Park Depot, also in 1976. (*Barry Lewis*)

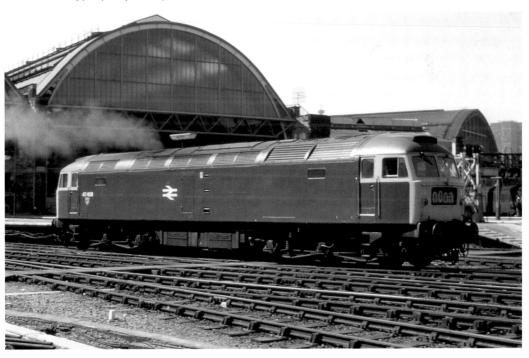

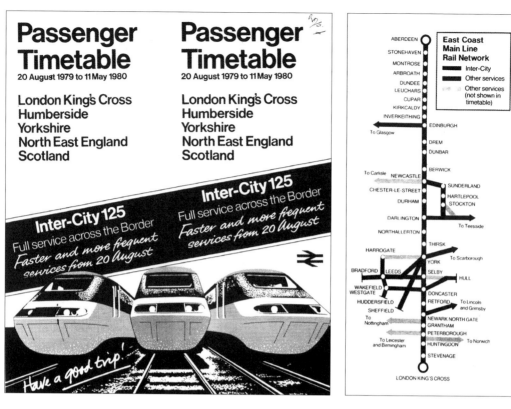

InterCity 125

Passenger timetable and route map for InterCity 125 High Speed Train services from King's Cross on the East Coast Main Line. The HSTs began working the Flying Scotsman expresses from the spring of 1978 and within a year had displaced the Deltics. Below, a clutch of HSTs peep out from the station.

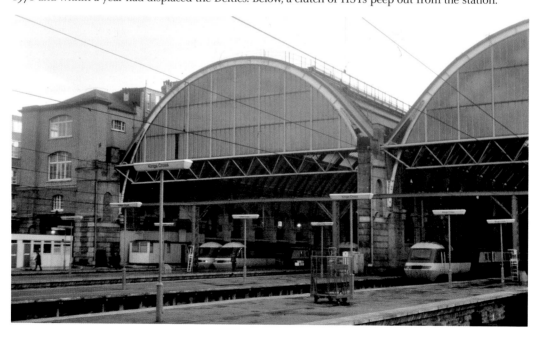

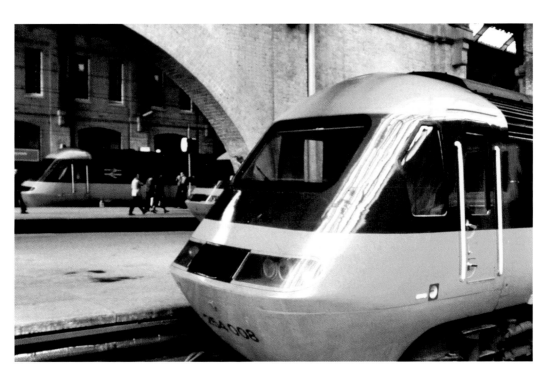

HST colours

The first British Railways HSTs had a startlingly modern look with the extended yellow and blue InterCity 125 colour scheme of the power cars. Above, looking through one of the central arches at King's Cross. The post-privatisation years have brought a far greater variety of colours, as shown in same view from 2012.

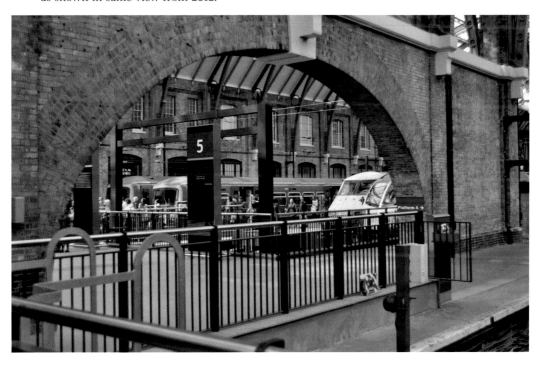

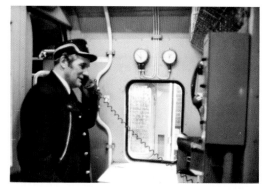
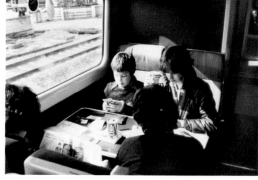
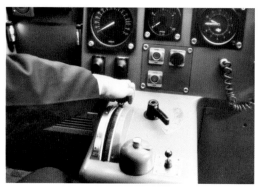
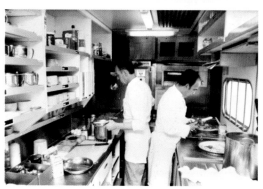

HST services

These photographs come from a series produced by British Railways Educational Services in the 1980s and were used in the training of staff on the East Coast Main Line. The HSTs have been operated by a number of other companies including GNER, National Express East Coast and by East Coast, photographed here in 2010.

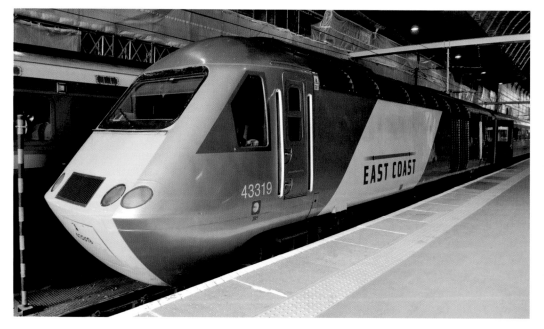

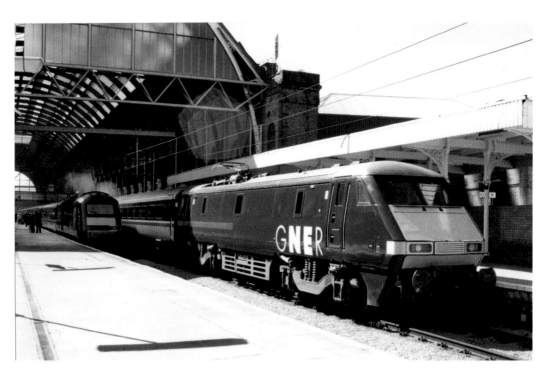

Class 91 and Class 180

An InterCity HST, 431117, loiters in the background while the GNER Class 91, 91012, emerges from the shadows at King's Cross in 1997. Below, the GNER livery has given way to the yellow and grey of East Coast on this Class 91. Standing next to it at Platform 5 is a Grand Central Class 180 Adelante.

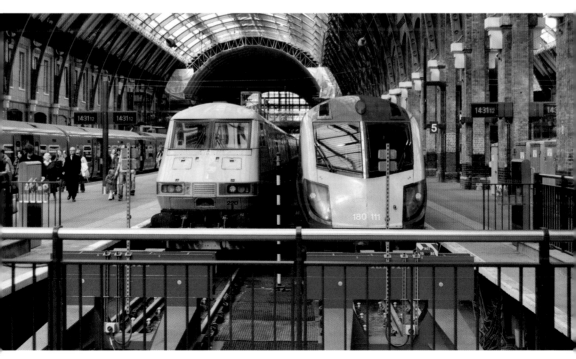

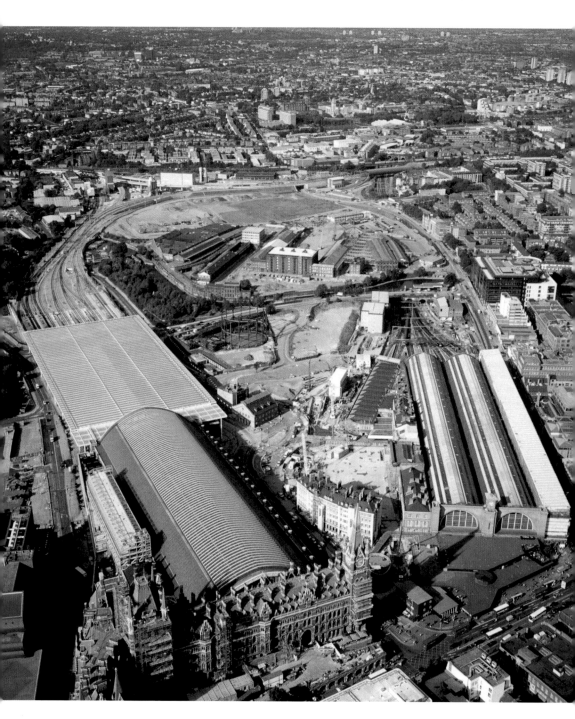

A superb aerial view of St Pancras and King's Cross showing the work in progress. A single gas holder remains standing, and beyond the canal is the Goods Yard with the Granary in the centre and Transit Sheds to either side. To the left are the long Coal Drops and the Western Goods Shed, to the right the Midland Shed with Handyside Roofs. (*Simon Hazelgrove/King's Cross Central*)

Goods Yard and Top Shed

It is said that each major station had its own distinctive smell, and for King's Cross that was the smell of coal. The Goods Yard at King's Cross, when combined with the adjoining Loco Depot, covered 59 acres of land immediately to the north of the station on the far side of the Regent's Canal. Its borders were defined by the canal and the Midland Railway line into St Pancras on the western side, Maiden Lane (now York Way) to the east and the North London Railway running across the top.

The scale and location of this Goods Yard so far into London made it an important transit point, feeding the capital's insatiable appetite for a number of commodities. The most important of these was coal from the north-eastern collieries which, until the coming of the railways, was exclusively delivered by sea-borne vessels travelling down the coast and into London via the Thames. The Great Northern Railway also provided greater access to inland collieries in the East Midlands and South Yorkshire. But it wasn't only coal; tons of grain, potatoes and perishable vegetables poured in from the rich farming counties including Lincolnshire, plus other fresh produce arrived daily such as fish from the North Sea fishing ports which could be on sale in the London markets in a matter of hours.

On the northern edge of the Goods Yard was the GNR's Locomotive Depot. Unlike the Goods Yard this area has been swept clean and no traces remain of the original crescent-shaped Locomotive Hall, the Erecting Shop and Running Shed, the Midland Railway's locomotive roundhouse – the MR shared part of the depot with the GNR for a time – and the coaling plant including the towering concrete hopper. Most of these buildings and structures survived until the 1960s but have now gone. Luckily, most of the buildings in the Goods Yard have survived, thanks largely to the depot's more gradual decline – primarily caused by the post-war growth in road transport – which has coincided with a greater appreciation of these solid industrial buildings and what they have to offer. The site at King's Cross is dominated by Lewis Cubitt's imposing 1851 Granary block and, as can be seen from the aerial photograph shown opposite, it is surrounded by various nineteenth-century buildings and structures including goods sheds, office buildings and the coal drops.

In their heyday the goods and loco depots were secure places only accessible to the hundreds of men who worked there, but at the start of the twenty-first century the surviving buildings are being restored in order to fulfil new roles as part of the exciting King's Cross Central regeneration plan.

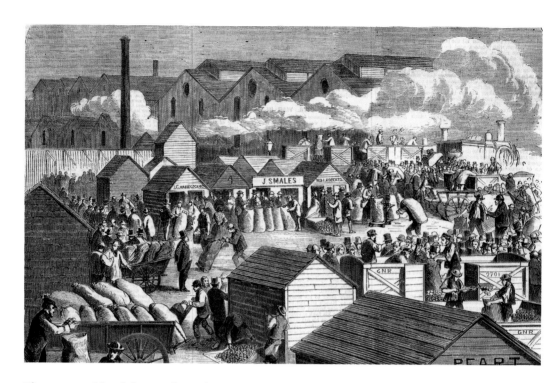

The eastern side of the Goods Yard

The potato market area was off Maiden Lane (York Way) and the merchants operated in the open air with just a collection of wooden huts to serve as their offices, shown in the *Illustrated London News* in 1864 before more permanent cover was provided. Below, the view from the canal bridge on York Way; the Granary on the left, the 1850 offices central and the later offices fronting the Midland Shed to the right. The main entrance to the yard was just to the north of the canal.

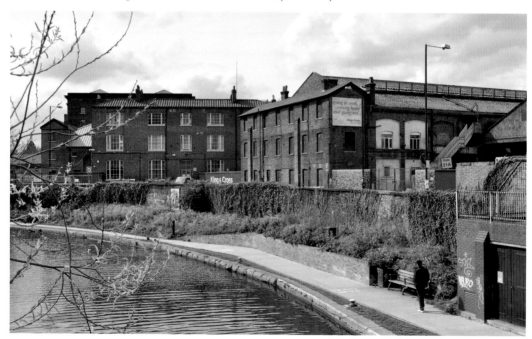

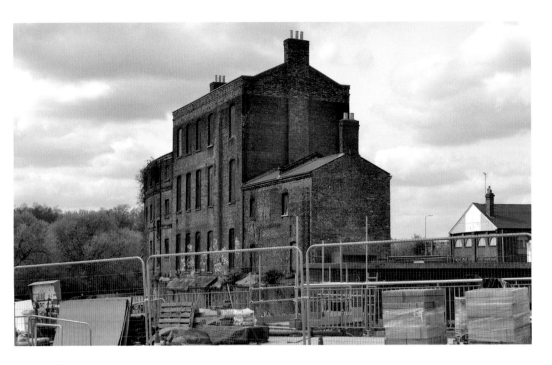

Office buildings

The assorted Fish and Coal Offices on Wharf Road which follow the curve of the canal, with the end of the Eastern Coal Drop to the right. Below, the newly restored 1850 offices between the Arrival Goods Shed and the Midland Shed – these are shown from the other side, left of centre, on the opposite page.

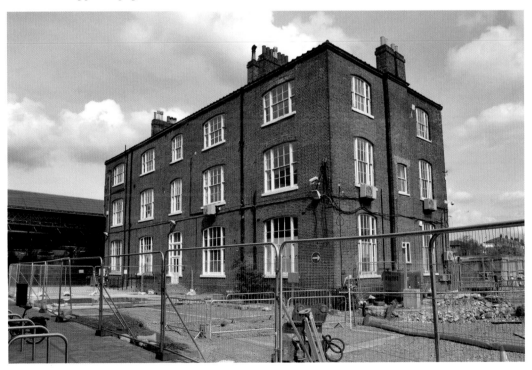

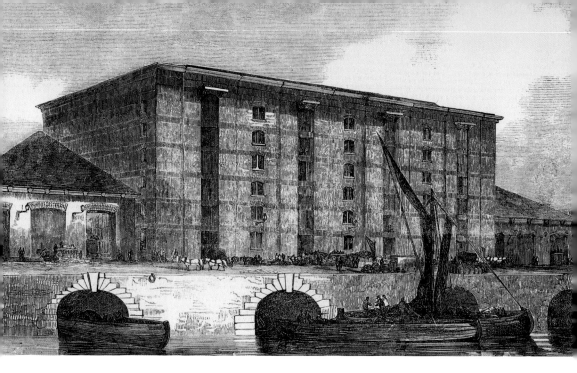

The 1851 Granary

Lewis Cubitt's six-storey Granary, which he asserted should be constructed in a 'plain, substantial manner'. It has openings for hoist access at the front, and slightly set back on either side are the two main Goods or Transit Sheds. Note the access tunnels which lead from a basin at the front of the building, now filled in. The Granary is part of the University of Arts London complex on the site.

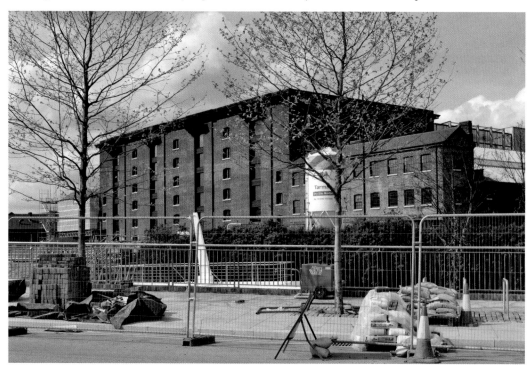

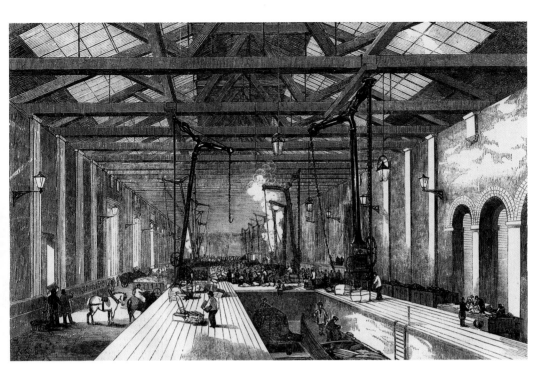

Transit Sheds

Interior view of the Western Transit Shed in 1853, showing horse-drawn carts on the left, the central platform with canal access and the railway to the right. Below, London Mayor Boris Johnson is shown the new atrium under construction between the back of the Granary and the sheds. (*John Sturrock/King's Cross Central*)

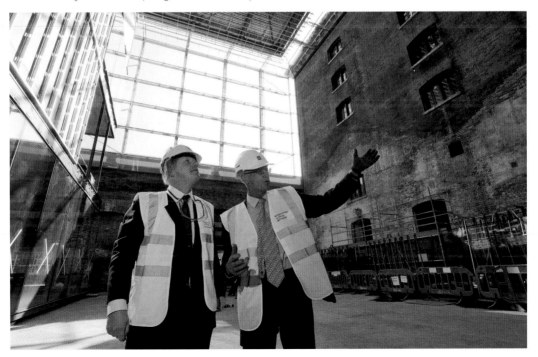

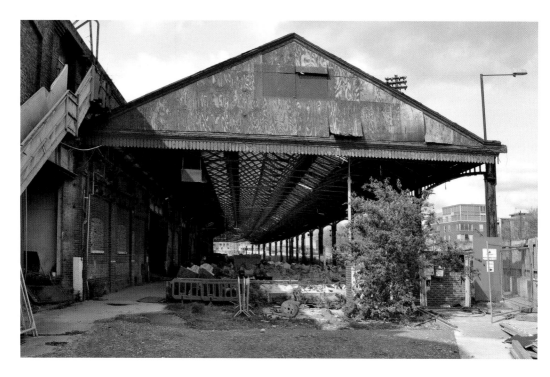

The 1888 Handyside Roofs

The temporary 1850 Maiden Lane Station stood on the eastern side, right, and this roof was constructed to fill the gap between it and the Midland Shed to provide better cover for the potato men. The old station has gone but some of the horizontal spandrels between the arches remain, visible on the right. See page 4.

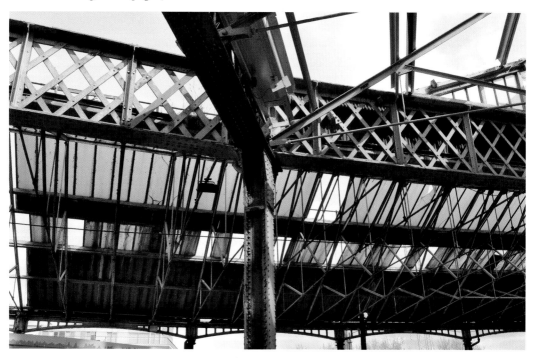

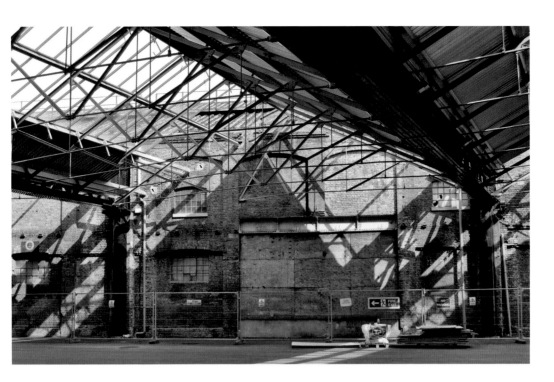

As with the roof on the opposite page, this was added in 1888 to fill the awkward space between the Midland Shed and Arrivals Transit Shed. These roofs are known as Handyside Roofs after the makers, Andrew Handyside & Co. Below, an impression of how the Coal Drops Yard area might look after the refurbishment has been completed. (*GMJ/King's Cross Central*)

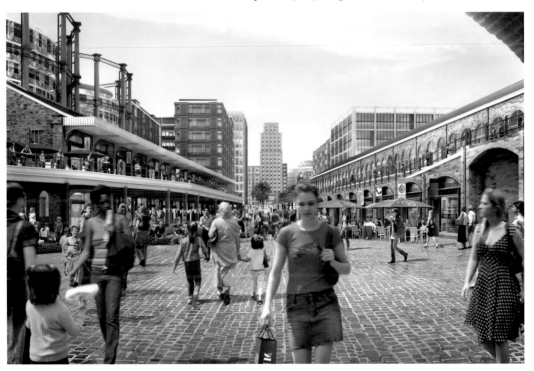

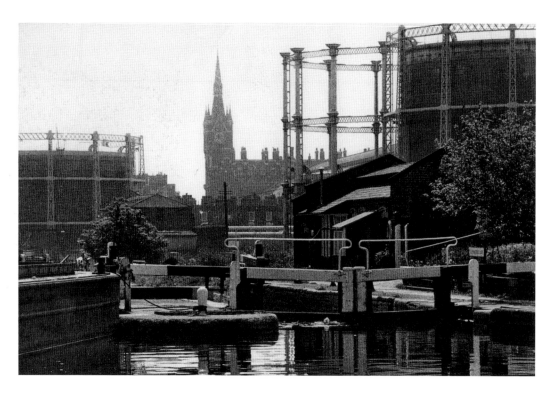

The Imperial Gas Light & Coke Company
Since 1824, long before the railways came, the gas company operated on land beside the canal.
At its height there were nine gas holders, the oldest from 1861, although gas production ceased in
1904. Photographed in 1975, above. The frames have been dismantled and await relocation. (*Bell
Phillips + Kimble/King's Cross Central*)

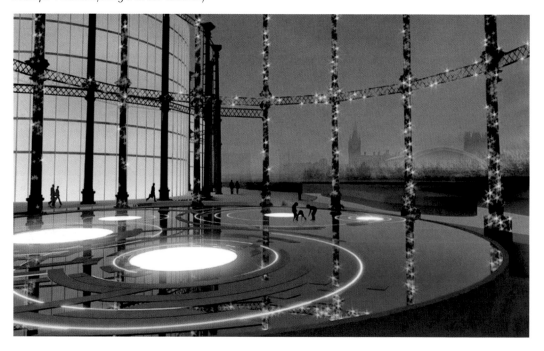

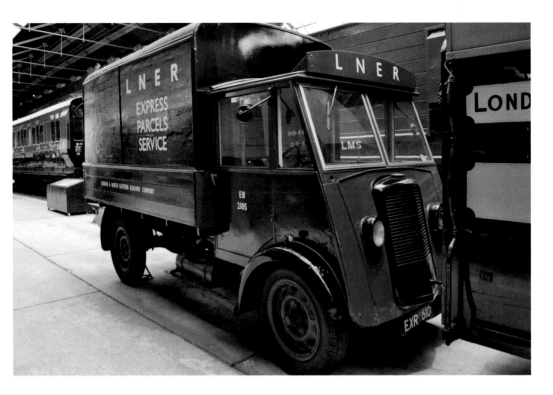

From rail to road

The LNER operated its own fleet of road vehicles including this 1938 Commer for the Express Parcels Service. Below, an interesting arrival at the Goods Yard in February 1935, a replica of Stephenson's *Rocket* is secured ready to be taken to the Science Museum. Note the Scammell Mechanical Horse in the background.

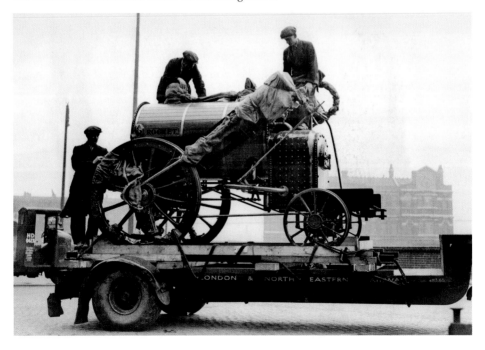

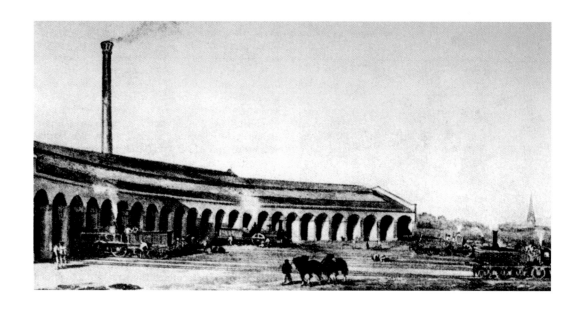

Curved and circular loco sheds

Above, the original GNR Locomotive Hall. Built in 1850, it had twenty-five spaces, each with its own door, plus an additional repair area at the back. It survived largely unchanged until the end of the steam era in 1963. Below, the Midland Roundhouse was built in 1859 on the north side of the GNR Loco Depot. Under an agreement with the GNR, the Midland Railway ran trains into King's Cross from 1858 and this arrangement included the construction of their own circular shed. It is shown here with a group of GNR suburban tank engines after the MR had vacated the site in 1868 for its own facilities on the far side of St Pancras. The Roundhouse was dismantled in 1931.

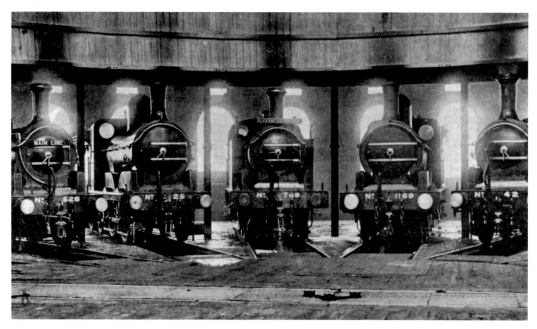

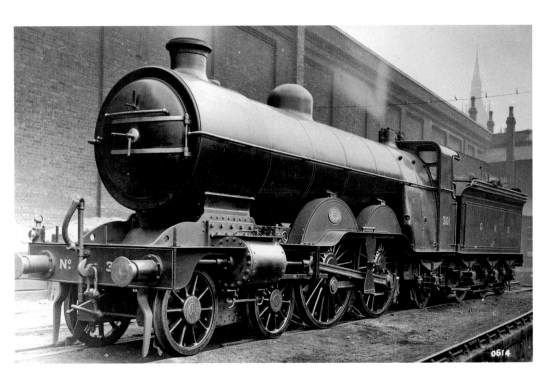

GNR locos

Above, GNR No 301, a Class C1 built between 1905 and 1907. It is shown in the Station Yard beside the Suburban Station, with the steeple of St Pancras in the background. Below, GNR No. 271, an Ivatt Class C2 Small Atlantic built in Doncaster in 1902, withdrawn in 1936 as LNER No. 3271.

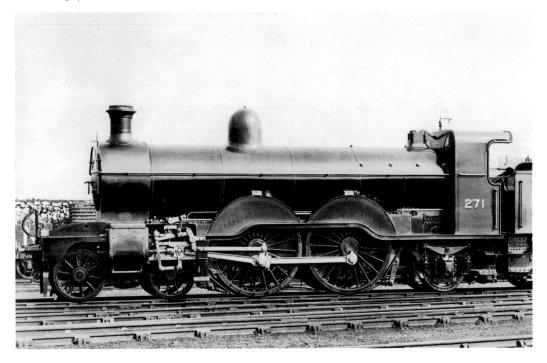

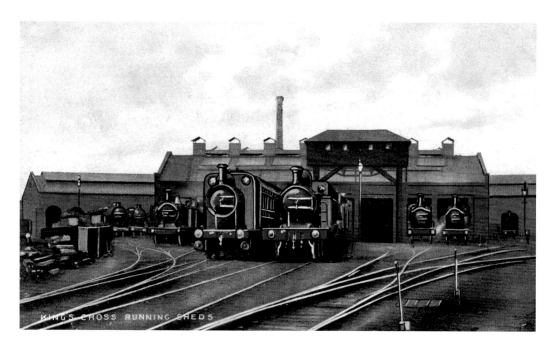

Main Line Running Shed

Postcard of the GNR's Running Shed *c.* 1905 with the curve of the original Locomotive Hall in the background. It was known as the Locomotive Cleaning Shed at first but later called the Main Line Running Shed, or Top Shed. Below: A 1950s photo taken from the coaling tower looking down on a busy Running Shed, with the old shed behind and St Pancras in the distance.

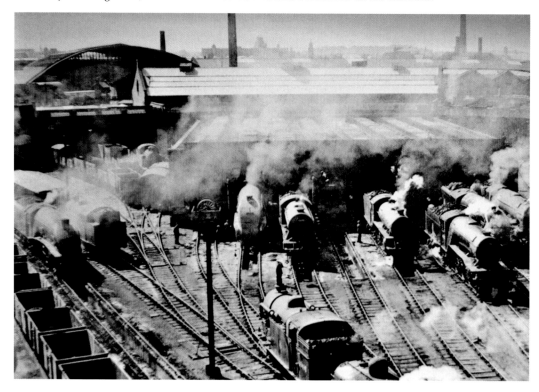

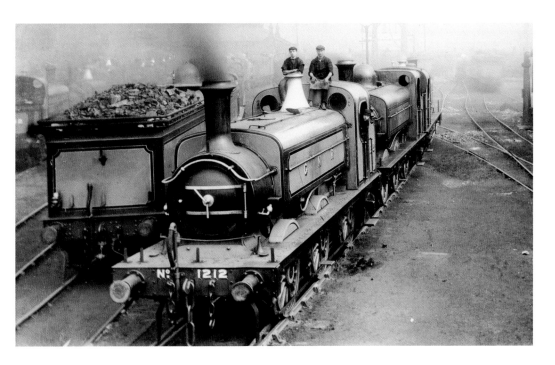

GNR Panniers

A pair of GNR Panniers. No. 1212 is at the front, in the ash-pit area with the Midland Railway Roundhouse just visible in the background on the left, and the hydraulic lift behind the second loco. Below, No. 1247, a J52 Class built in 1899, photographed at the NRM's facility at Shildon in County Durham.

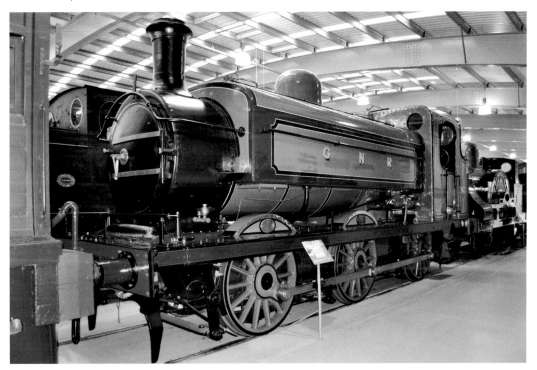

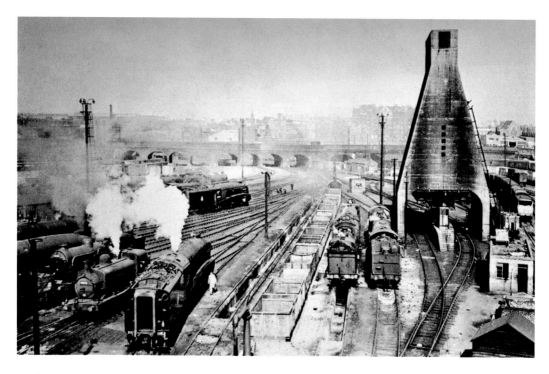

Coaling Plant

Loco depot looking east with the Maiden Lane bridge arches in the distance and the concrete Coaling Plant or Tower with wagon hoist on the right. With the advent of the diesels it was no longer needed and was demolished in 1964. (*CMcC*)

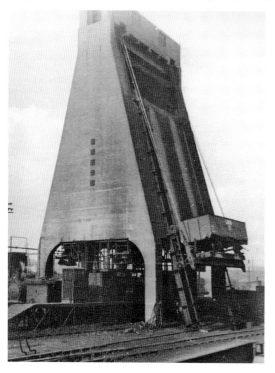

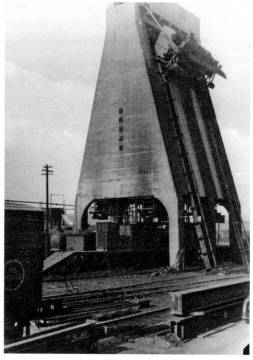

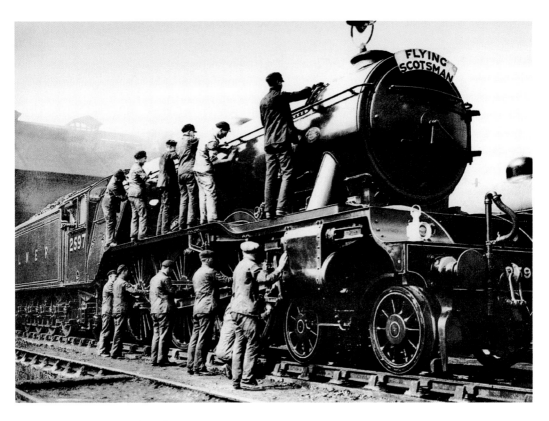

LNER *Gainsborough* **and** *Green Arrow*

A pre-war publicity photograph showing a team of cleaners at work polishing No. 2597 *Gainsborough* in front of the Top Shed. This was an LNER Gresley Class A1/A3, later renumbered as 60086 for BR and withdrawn in 1963. Below, No. 4771 *Green Arrow*, a Class V2 built in 1936 and now displayed at the NRM.

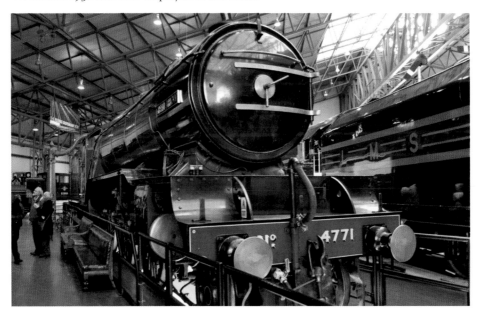

Change at King's Cross

It is a minor miracle that King's Cross Station has survived for 160 years virtually unspoilt. Over that time there has been a procession of schemes to alter the station, usually with the intention of improving the restricted concourse area or, in some cases, giving Lewis Cubitt's façade a complete makeover. The LNER had radical plans for replacing the front of the station with new offices, shown below. In the latter half of the twentieth century planners switched their focus to creating a new linking concourse area between King's Cross and St Pancras, in some cases involving the demolition of the Great Northern Hotel. British Rail's answer was to build a 'temporary' single-storey extension at the front of the station to accommodate the booking hall. But the greatest impetus to change came in 2005 with the announcement of a £500 million refurbishment programme that has successfully preserved the historic buildings by sensitively introducing the best elements of modern design. The main component of this has been a new concourse designed by John McAslan to fill the semi-circular area between the hotel and the western side of the station. The result is spectacular. In its re-born form King's Cross has managed to retain its strong individuality with its architectural integrity intact. It has finally emerged from the shadows of St Pancras.

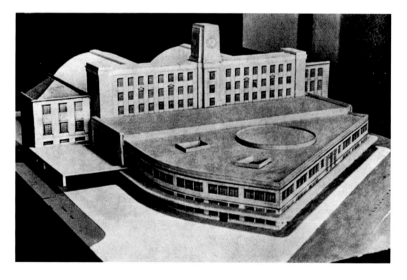

LNER's plans for the post-war King's Cross included remodelling the front to create office space, but only loosely retained the spirit of Lewis Cubitt's original.

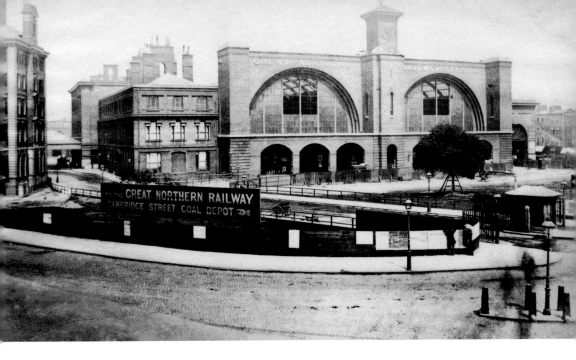

All change at King's Cross?

Above, a very early photograph of the station frontage with the forecourt still clear of the 'village' of assorted hutments. Note the sign for the GNR Cambridge Street Coal Depot and the gated road leading to the main entrance canopy beside the offices. The corner of the Great Northern Hotel is on the far left. Apart from the 1970s canopy, the newly refurbished station looks remarkably like the original.

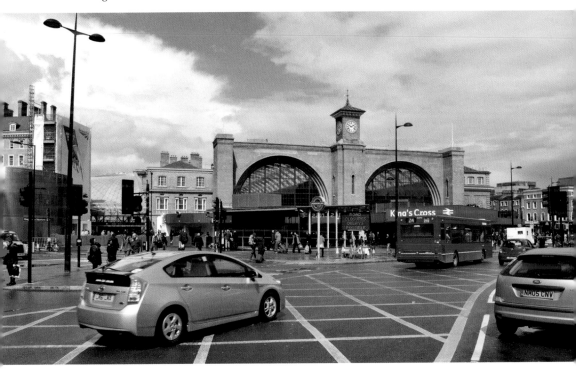

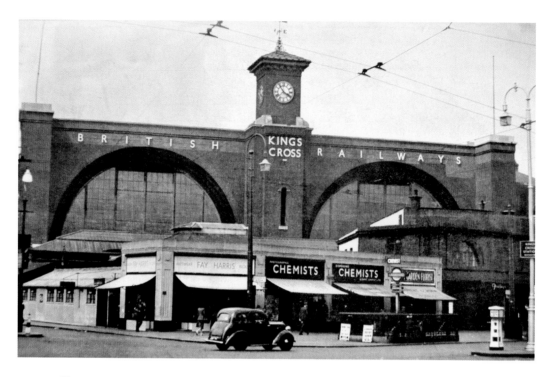

Half a century ahead of its time

A pair of images from a 1952 centenary proposal to 'revive the grandeur of the building'. The upper photograph is of interest for the detail it reveals of the shops and the Underground Station – see p87 – while the visualisation of a de-cluttered frontage anticipates the current plans with extraordinary accuracy.

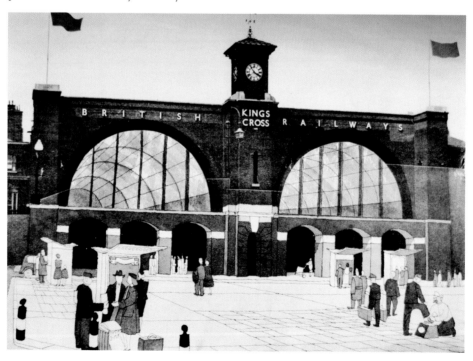

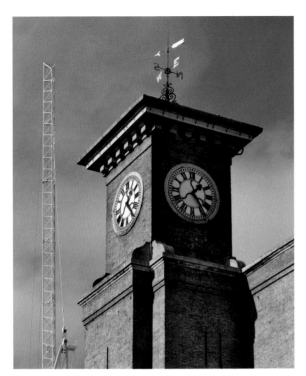
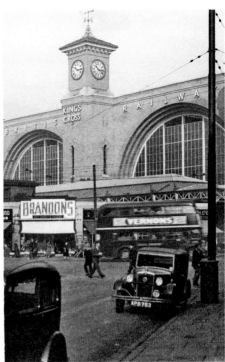

The one concession to ornament is the Italianate clock turret. The four-faced clock was made by Dent of London and had been displayed at the 1851 Great Exhibition before installation at King's Cross (since replaced by an electronic mechanism). Above left, in 1953, and below, in the 1980s with the BR canopy in black. You can make out where the lettering had been.

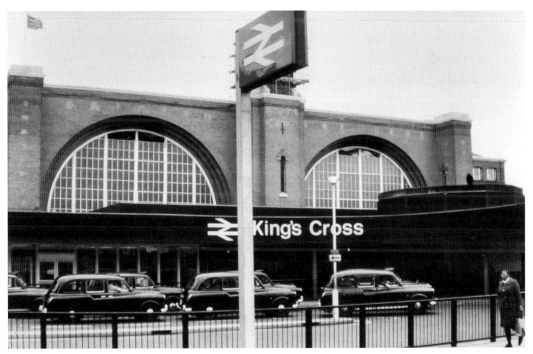

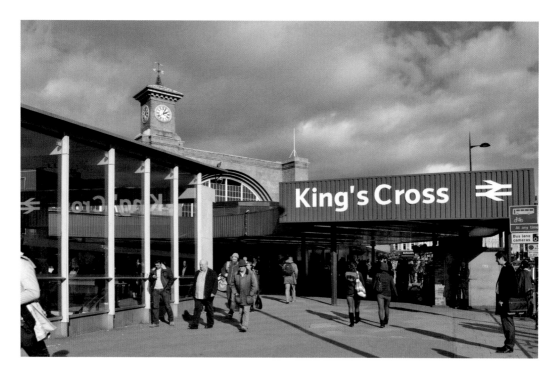

A temporary extension, forty years on

Photographed in 2010, the canopy extension was erected by British Rail in 1972 to provide additional concourse space, including a new booking hall, shown below in this 1980s photo and opposite. The temporary extension is awaiting demolition as part of the £500 million restoration plan announced by NetworkRail in 2005.

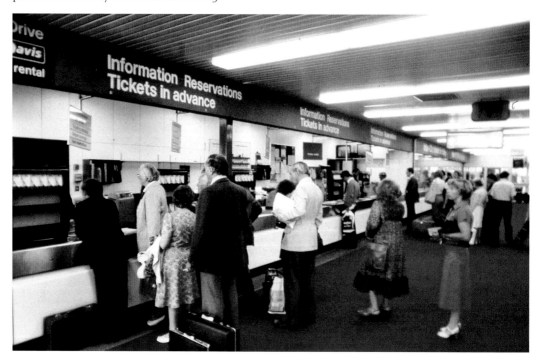

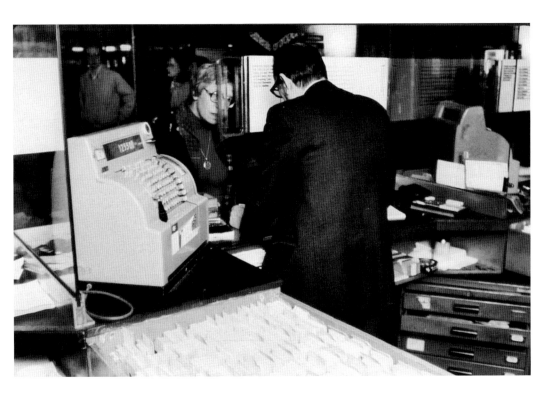

Booking Hall facilities within the extension
Inside the Booking Office in the 1980s. Note the huge till and rack of tickets. Below, travellers crowd around the destination board, 2010. This Booking Hall has been superseded by the spacious new Western Concourse – see p80–82.

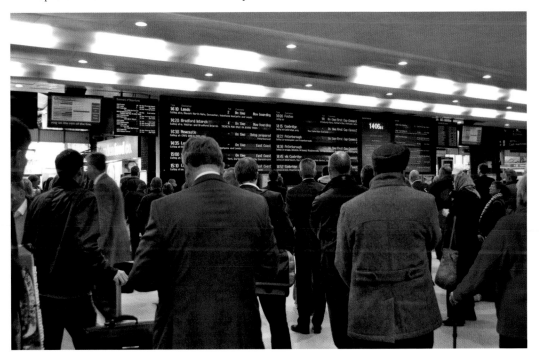

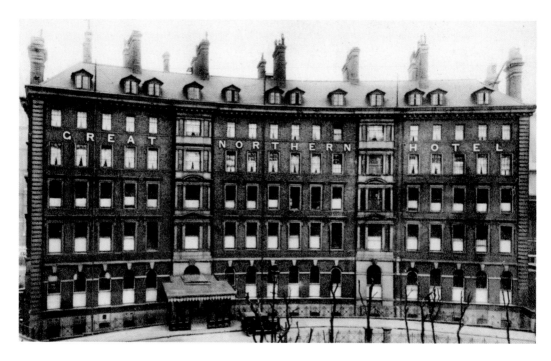

The Great Northern Hotel

Once faced with demolition, thankfully the Great Northern Hotel has been refurbished and incorporated within the new station concourse. It was built in a curve to follow the line of the road. Originally a garden filled the space between hotel and station. Below, in 2009. (*John Sturrock/Kings Cross Central*)

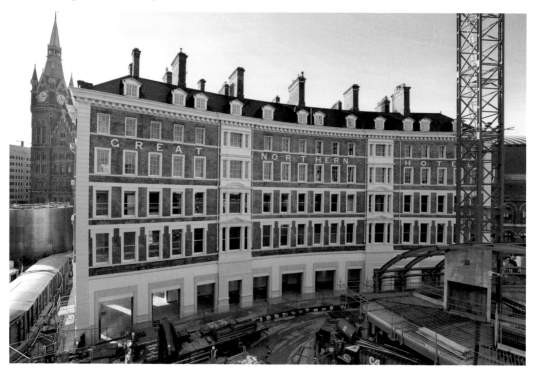

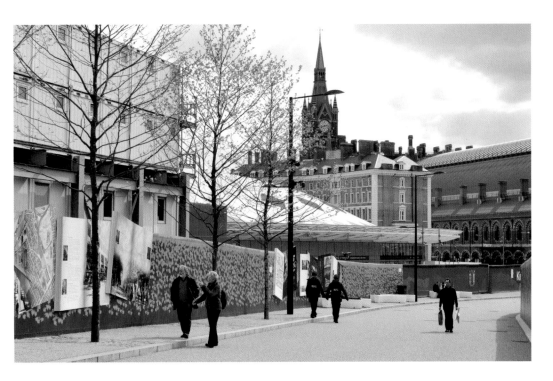

Between stations

Above, looking back towards the hotel and St Pancras from Battle Bridge Road. It is planned to complete the refurbishment in time to re-open the hotel before the London Olympics. Below, seen from Euston Road side in the spring of 2012.

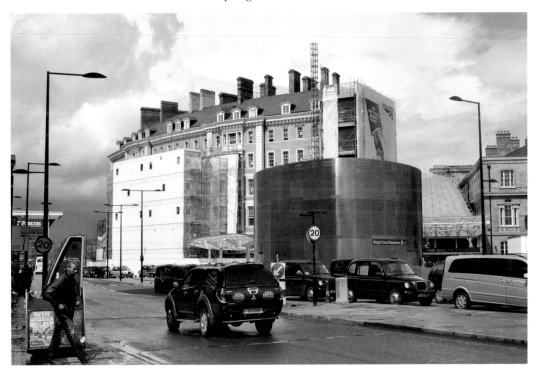

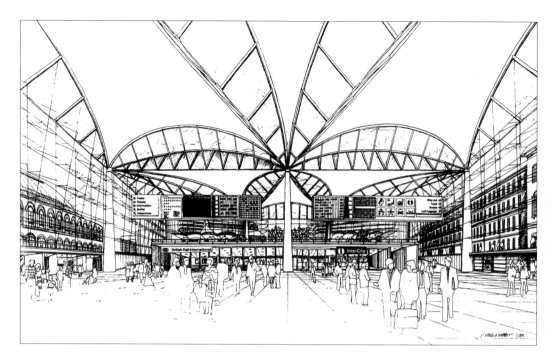

Linking the stations

Over the decades there have been many proposals to link the two stations with a new concourse. This late 1980s scheme envisaged knocking down the hotel and erecting a glass-clad triangle, shown here looking north with St Pancras on the left and King's Cross to the right. Below, the southern entrance into the new Western Concourse shortly after it was opened in March 2012.

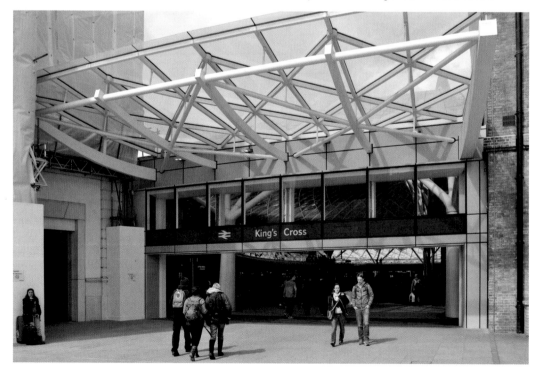

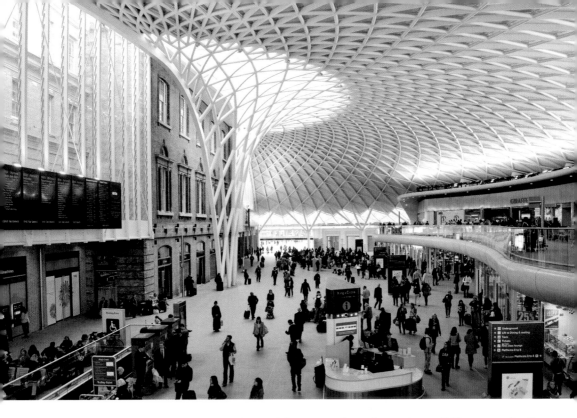

John McAslan has created a semi-circular roof that erupts from the station wall like a cascade of steel and glass and flows into the curve of the hotel building.

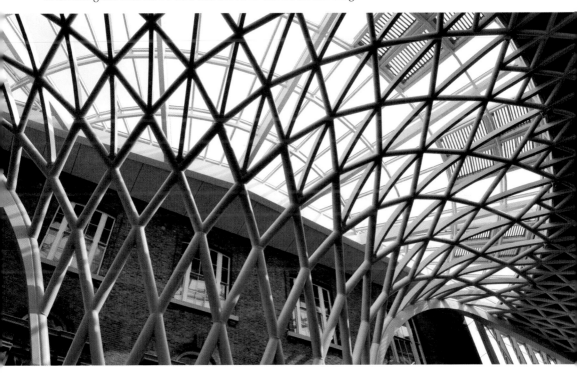

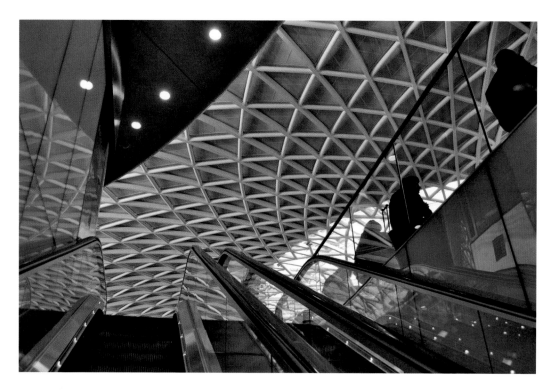

The new concourse

Going up the escalator to the mezzanine, the intricate structure of 1,200 solid and 1,012 glass panels changes colour, almost imperceptibly. The concourse is designed to cope with around 100,000 travellers passing through at peak times.

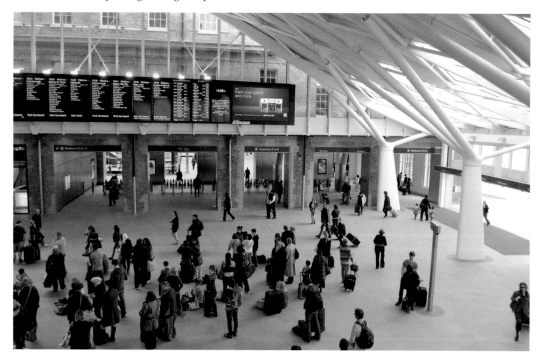

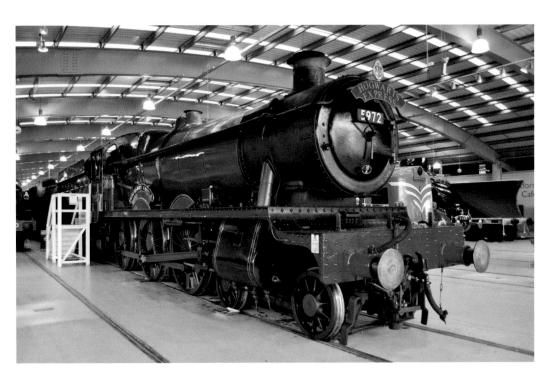

Pottering about

As everyone knows, the Hogwarts Express departed from Platform 9¾ at King's Cross. *Hogwarts Castle*, aka *Olton Hall* GWR No. 5972, is shown at the NRM Shildon. The disappearing trolley used to be at the end of the suburban platforms, but has been moved to the new concourse where Potter fans queue up for a photo.

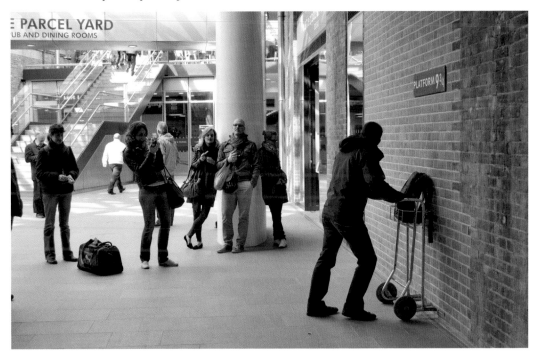

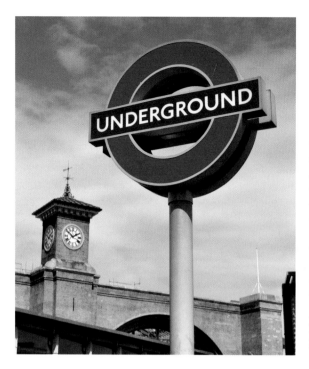

The latest Underground sign to appear at King's Cross. The distinctive 'wheel-and-bar' roundel was originally adopted from the London General Omnibus Company and later applied by London Transport to all surface and underground services.

Below, 1903 rail map with the King's Cross area to the right. Note the Suburban and York Road stations linking with the Metropolitan Railway, which is shown in dark brown.

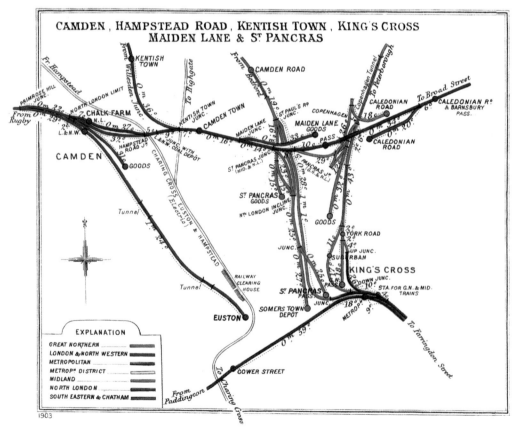

CAMDEN, HAMPSTEAD ROAD, KENTISH TOWN, KING'S CROSS MAIDEN LANE & St PANCRAS

1903

King's Cross Connections

As stations go, the King's Cross St Pancras combination – in terms of the Underground it is regarded as one station – is very well connected. It is currently served by more lines than any other, six in all: the Hammersmith & City Line, the Circle Line, the Metropolitan, the Northern, the Piccadilly and the Victoria Line. After Waterloo and Victoria it is the third busiest station on the London Underground.

The first line to reach King's Cross had been the Metropolitan Railway, which opened in 1863 with a station on Pentonville Road. The Great Northern, Piccadilly & Brompton Railway (now part of the Piccadilly Line) opened its station building in front of King's Cross in 1906, plus another one on York Road (York Way) to the north. The most recent arrival was the Victoria Line, which came into operation at King's Cross & St Pancras in 1968.

More recently, two very different events have had a direct impact on the Underground station. The first was the tragic fire in November 1987 which killed thirty-one people and highlighted the need to update and improve access underground. It is thought that a cigarette may have fallen into an escalator machine room and, consequently, the old wooden steps on the escalators were replaced by metal ones. The second event was the decision to make St Pancras the new terminus for the Eurostar international service, the so-called High Speed 1, and the major redevelopment of the station complex included an extensive remodelling and upgrading of the Underground facilities. Completed in 2009, these improvements included an expanded Main Ticket Hall at the front of King's Cross, the Western Ticket Hall which is located beneath the forecourt of the St Pancras hotel, and the Northern Ticket Hall constructed beneath the new concourse area on the western side of King's Cross. Between them these facilities are served by a bewildering number of entrances from both of the main line stations, inside and outside, and on the streets in the immediate area. The original Metropolitan Railway station on Pentonville Road became the King's Cross Thameslink station in 1988, and although it is now disused public access to King's Cross & St Pancras remains open from there via one of the longest pedestrian tunnels on the system.

What's in a name

Should King's Cross be written with or without an apostrophe? The area is usually without, the station with, although station signage has vacillated between both versions over the years.

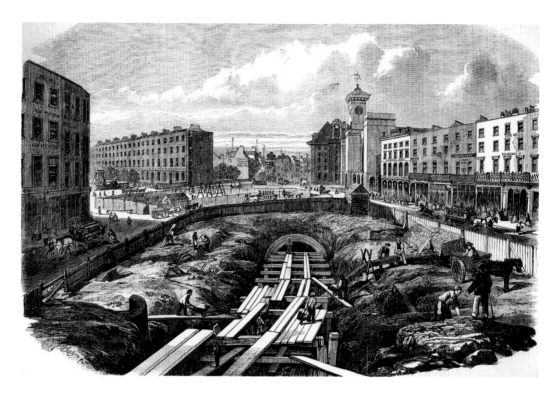

Building the Metropolitan Railway

This 1861 engraving graphically illustrates the disruption caused by the cut-and-cover method of construction favoured by the Metropolitan Railway. Note the absence of St Pancras in this view along the Pentonville Road towards King's Cross. Below, seen from almost the same spot today. Love the Police three-wheeler.

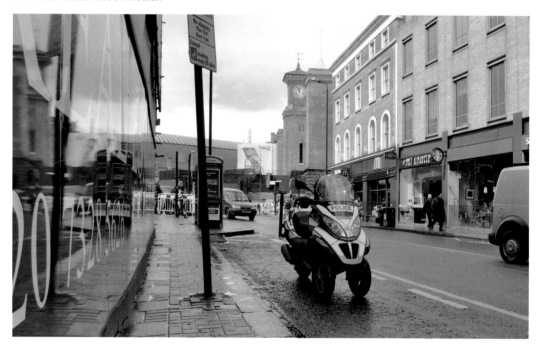

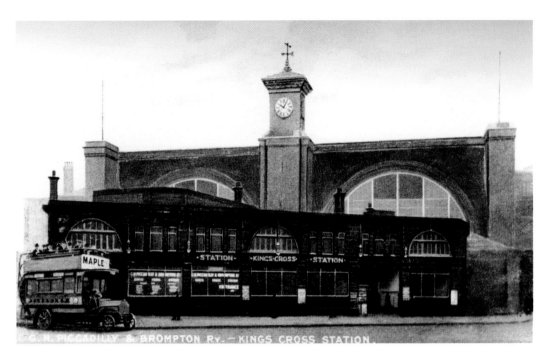

Great Northern, Piccadilly & Brompton Railway

The GNP&BR stations at the front of King's Cross, above, and the York Road station (not to be confused with the York Road Platform for suburban trains) on the corner of Bingfield Street and what is now York Way. Both opened in 1906, and both feature Leslie Green's distinction ox-blood red tiles and semi-circular over-windows. The GNP&BR later became the Piccadilly Line. York Road closed in 1932 although the surface building and platforms remain and there are suggestions that it could be re-opened to serve the King's Cross Central development area. The GNP&BR station building at the front of King's Cross has gone.

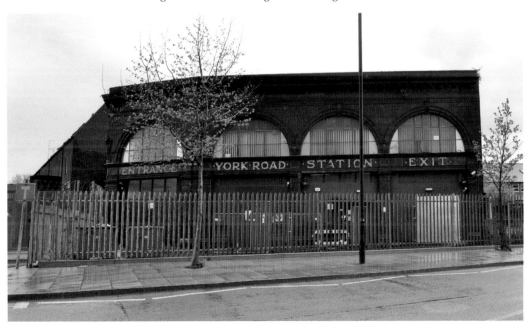

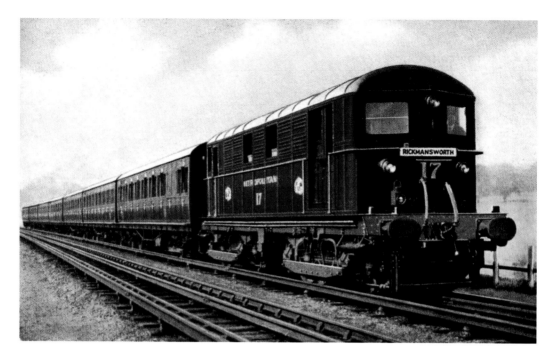

Metropolitan Railway

The electrification of the locomotives solved the smoke issue and was an important factor in the expansion of the Underground network, including the construction of deeper lines. Above, Metropolitan Railway's No. 17, a Vickers Electric Locomotive, and below, No. 10 the *William Ewart Gladstone* with destination board for Aldgate. A preserved example can be seen at the TfL Museum in Covent Garden.

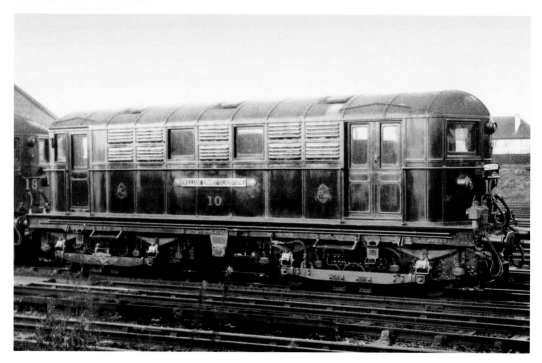

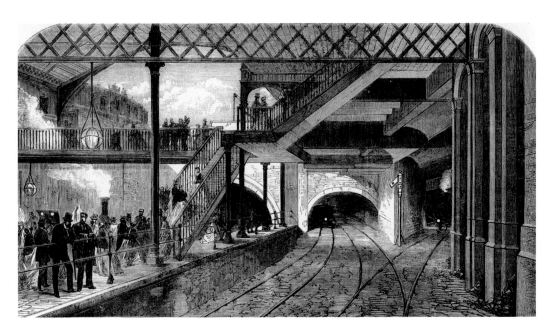

Multiple connections

A 1868 print from the *Illustrated London News* showing the junction of the Great Northern Railway and the Metropolitan Railway at King's Cross. The Metropolitan's station is on the left. Today the King's Cross & St Pancras Underground station is the biggest interchange station on the underground network and is serviced by six tube lines. In 2006 London Underground completed the refurbishment of the Western Ticket Hall, below, which is located underneath the forecourt of the St Pancras Hotel.

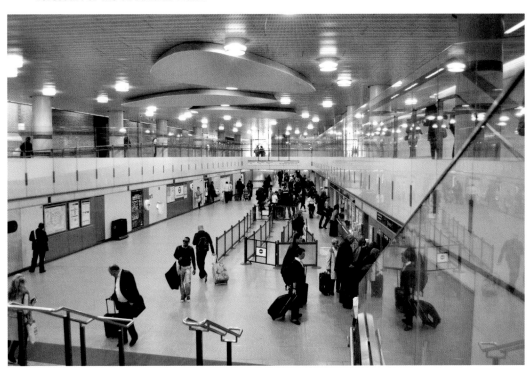

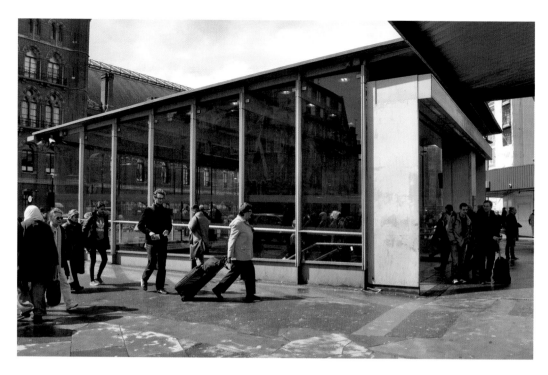

King's Cross & St Pancras Underground Station

Two modern entrances down to the joint King's Cross & St Pancras Underground Station. Above, at the front of the main King's Cross Station on the corner of Euston Road and Pancras Road, and below on the north side of the new King's Cross concourse.

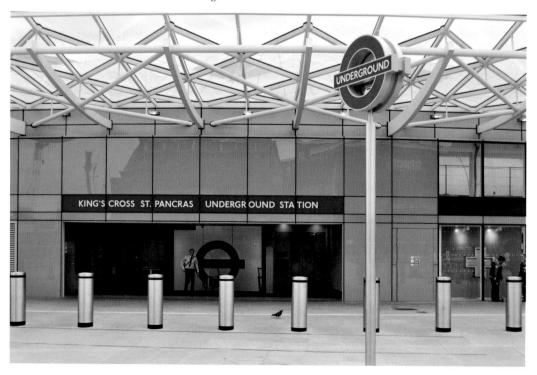

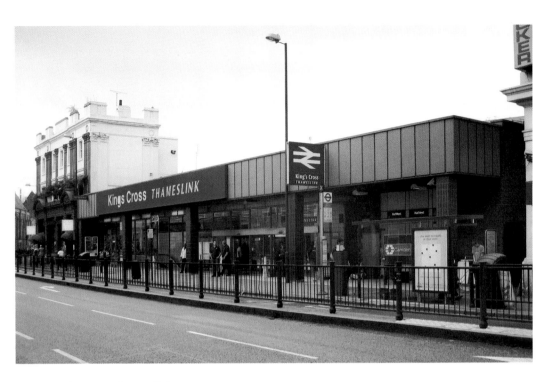

King's Cross Thameslink

The station on the south side of Pentonville Road occupied part of the former 1863 Metropolitan Railway site. The platforms were on the Widened Lines and served the Metropolitan, Circle and Hammersmith and City Lines until 1979. The station reopened in 1983 as King's Cross Midland City and in 1988 became King's Cross Thameslink, shown above. This service continued until December 2007, when new Thameslink platforms opened beneath St Pancras. (*Gary Houston*)

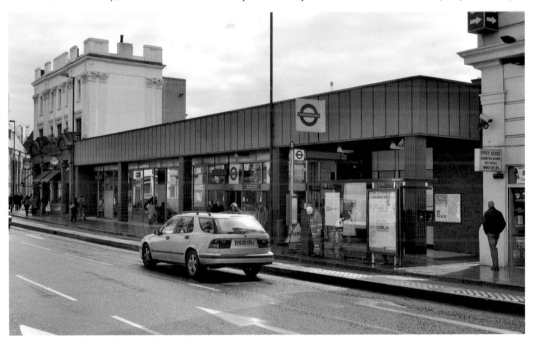

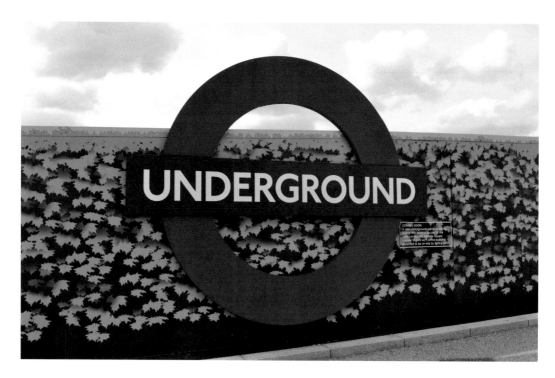

A sign of things to come

This hoarding indicates the position of a new Underground entrance north of Battle Bridge Road on the edge of the B2 plot between the two stations. Behind the hoardings this big hole is the start of the Pancras Square development, a sign that there are many changes yet to come with the King's Cross Central scheme. Looking back towards the German Gymnasium and remains of Stanley Buildings.

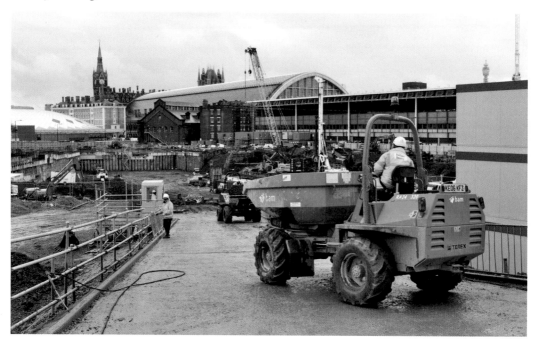

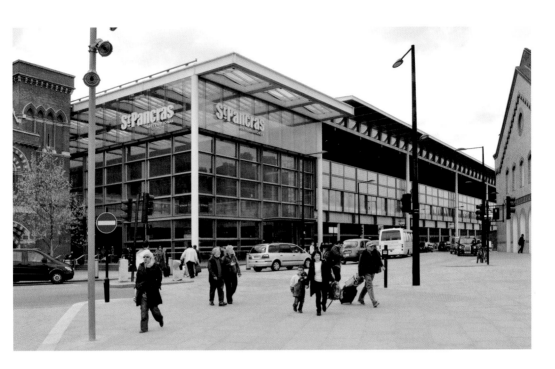

Close neighbours

East entrance to St Pancras International, which was officially opened by the Queen on 6 November 2007. Eurostar services commenced one week later. Below, the German Gymnasium, built in 1865 for the German Gymnastic Society, features laminated wooden ribs similar to those used in the original King's Cross roofs.

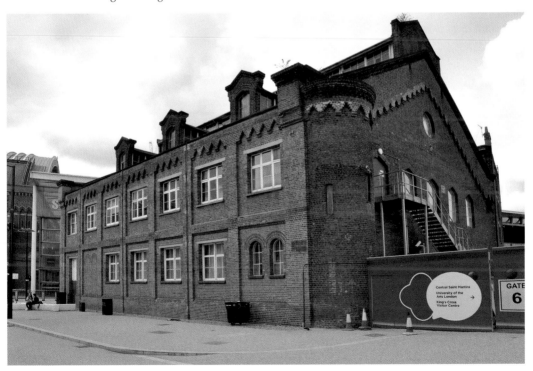

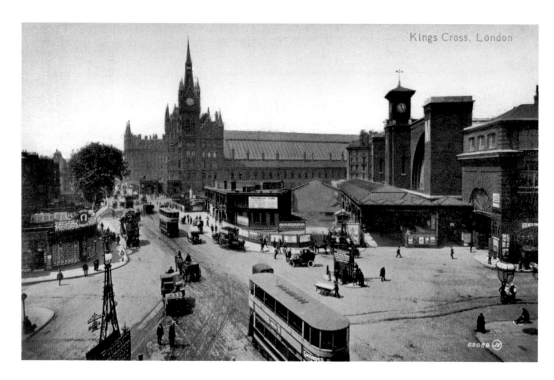

St Pancras Station and Midland Grand Hotel

The showy neighbour, George Gilbert Scott's highly decorative hotel façade, all points and pinnacles, is in sharp contrast to the functionality of King's Cross. Above, looking westwards along Euston Road *c.* 1905. Note the 'Piccadilly Tube' station under construction, and assorted buildings and the canopy at the front of King's Cross.

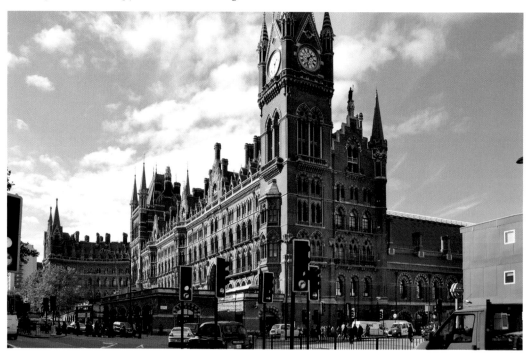

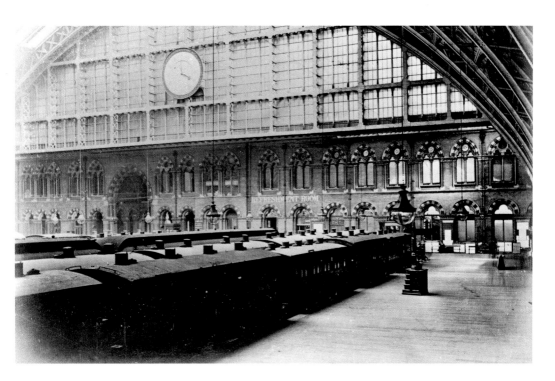

A statue of Sir John Betjeman stands in St Pancras, eyes perpetually raised to Barlow's magnificent Train Shed roof. Betjeman is widely credited as the saviour of St Pancras; he was an avid admirer of Victorian railway architecture at a time when it was largely out of favour. But is St Pancras better than King's Cross?

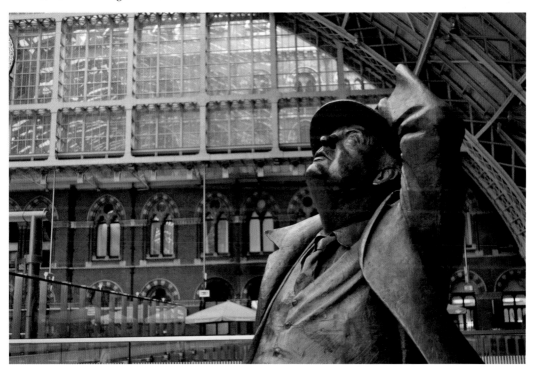

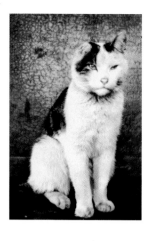

The Goods Yard cat
This fine chap is George, the battle-scarred King's Cross Goods Yard moggie who was enough of a celebrity to have his photograph put on a postcard. You don't want to mess with George. There is a tradition of station cats at London's big termini, but that must be the subject for another book.

Further reading

Change at King's Cross, Michael Hunter and Robert Thorne (editors), Historical Publications 1990.
The Great British Railway Stations: King's Cross, Chris Hawkins, Irwell Press 1990.
King's Cross in the Twenties, by W. Rayner Thrower, The Oakwood Press 1978.
King's Cross Renaissance, P. W. B. Semmens, Railway Magazine supplement, 1990.
Railway Lands – Catching St Pancras and King's Cross, Angela Inglis, Matador 2007.
Top Shed – A Pictorial History of King's Cross Locomotive Depot, P. N. Townend, Ian Allan 1975.
The Transformation of St Pancras Station, Lansley, Durant, Dyke, Gambrill and Shelton, Laurence King Publishing 2007/2012.

Other titles in this series by John Christopher:
Paddington Station Through Time
Victoria Station Through Time
Euston Station Through Time
plus *Isambard Kingdom Brunel Through Time*

Acknowledgements

I would like to thank Campbell McCutcheon (*CMcC*) of Amberley Publishing for commissioning this book and for supplying several of the images from his extensive collection of old postcards. For additional images I am grateful to NetworkRail, Michael J. Irlam, Steel City Ady, Lewis Collard, Phil Sangwell, Dave John, Barry Lewis, Gary Houston and Colourrail. King's Cross Central images by GMI, John Sturrock, Simon Hazelgrove and Bell Phillips + Kimble. Unless otherwise credited, all new photography is by the author (*JC*). Special thanks to the extremely helpful staff at King's Cross Station.

And finally...
The story goes that in 1936 Wallis Simpson took a taxi from her London residence to catch a train for a weekend up north. 'King's Cross,' she said to the driver. 'I'm sorry to hear that, madam,' came the reply.